Praise for
The Mommy Diaries

If you are in the market for a fancy, high-browed look at parenting, put this book down. If you are looking for hilarious and brutally honest accounts of what every mother is secretly dealing with, read on. Dallas tells the good, the bad, and the poopy in this vulnerable account of a real-life modern mother/ housewife/domestic goddess just trying to make it through another day. I wish all books could be this refreshing!

> —KERRI POMAROLLI, Actress (*NBC, Lifetime, ABC Family*); Comedian; Author of *Guys Like Girls Named Jennie*; Mom

Dallas Louis clearly demonstrates her understanding of the challenges and rewards that parenting can bring. Through humorous illustrations, real-life application, and a dose of reality, Dallas reminds us that while "parenting is not for sissies," our Heavenly Father can be trusted to guide us every step of the way—even when that step involves "Legos."

> —SHANNON PERRY, Author of *Grace in High Heels*; Recording Artist/Speaker/M.Ed.

The Mommy Diaries is a refreshing look at the everyday things of life. Dallas Louis does not sugarcoat the genuine bugaboos of mommyhood. She writes freely about her personal struggles with the daily grind and offers useful, workable perspectives on family issues. In the middle of life's craziness, Dallas finds a secure center in God and His wise and wonderful plan. If you're feeling overwhelmed or discouraged with how things are going in your home, or if you are just generally looking for hope, encouragement, laughter, or direction at this point in your family life, this book is for you!

—Rev. Dr. Richard C. Noack, Senior Pastor, Trinity
Klein Lutheran Church, Spring, Texas

I just love Dallas—God's truth with just a spoonful of hazelnut syrup to make it go down in the best way. If you need someone to help you get through the day, make sure you take a double helping of her wit and wisdom.

—Kathi Lipp, Speaker and Author of *The Husband Project*
and *The What's for Dinner? Solution*

I have been a fan of Dallas' work since I laughed all the way through her one-month-devotional book *Girlfriends, Giggles, & God* last year. I have been waiting with baited breath for her name to appear on another book, and when I had the pleasure of reading *The Mommy Diaries*, it came as no big surprise that I found myself laughing out loud at yet another of her blatantly honest and revealing exposés. As a mom with only minimal practice in raising children myself, I found my suspicions confirmed, my fears relieved, my gut feelings about questionable modern parenting theories strengthened, and somewhere along the way I was reminded that even the most stressful and frightening challenges in life can be a fun learning experience. Thank you again, Dallas, for bringing hilarity and smiles in a very scary world to a fairly new mom.

—Donna Lee Howell, Successful Ghostwriter; Author
of *Ebenezer: The Final Years of Scrooge*; Contributing
Author of *God's Ghostbusters: Vampires? Ghosts? Aliens?
Werewolves? Creatures of the Night Beware!*

THE MOMMY DIARIES
HOW I'M SURVIVING PARENTING
WITHOUT KILLING ANYONE

DALLAS LOUIS

ANOMALOS PUBLISHING HOUSE

CRANE

The Mommy Diaries:
How I'm Surviving Parenting without Killing Anyone

HighWay: A division of Anomalos Publishing
Crane, MO 65633

Printed in the United States of America
12 1

ISBN 13: 9780983621669

Cover design by Shim Franklin

A CIP catalog record of this book is available from the Library
of Congress.

Dedication

This book is dedicated to my parents, Jonathan and Lucretia Doyer. Without the foundation that I was given at home, I would have had no hope of succeeding in life. You taught me the importance of discipline (though I despised *it* and *you* at the time), how to clean a bathroom, how to read a recipe, and most importantly, you showed me what love looked like through every stage of parenting—even when the child was unlovable. Mother and Daddy, I love you.

To my husband, Jeff, and our three totally awesome kids: without y'all, I couldn't have even written this book! Jeff, you have been my partner in parenting, my nurse (at times), my lover, and you continue to be the love of my life. Though we may not always see eye-to-eye, we always stand side-by-side. I love you. Kids: I couldn't have handpicked any better kids, even if I'd ordered you from a catalog! I love each of you so much. Thank you for enjoying life, and simply loving the way God made you.

Acknowledgements

There are a number of people I want to thank for helping with the creative process of *The Mommy Diaries*.

Mother: Thank you for reading every thought, word, and page that I sent to you...including the ones that didn't make any sense at all! Your constant support kept me writing when I would've rather stopped.

Jean: You've been a well-spring of encouragement... always. Thank you for reading the really "rough" rough drafts, and for helping me make them better. Thank you for helping to make *me* better.

Suzanne: Thank you for all of your support, encouragement, and critique. You provided me with a fresh perspective on words I'd been looking at for so long that they were beginning to blur together! Your insight was just what I needed! Thank you.

Shannon: Girl! Where do I even begin? Amidst your crazy-busy and hectic schedule (recording, TV shows, speaking... I'm tired just thinking about your appointment calendar!), I handed you a book, and asked you to read it. Thank you for your kind words! Whatever you are juggling in your world, you always make time for others. Thank you, my friend.

Kerri: Thank you for making me spit tea out of my nose! When I read your review of *The Mommy Diaries*, I had a mouthful of sweet tea...thus spraying my kitchen! Thank you for always making me laugh. And thank you for suffering through the "unedited version" to get to heart of this book!

Pastor Noack: Your words made me cry. I'll just state that right up front. Thank you so much for *always* listening, *always* praying, *always* helping...*always* just being there. You are an irreplaceable source of information, motivation, and peace in my life. Thank you for your wisdom and for your kind words of encouragement.

Kathi: Not only did you read *The Mommy Diaries*, but you offered such kind and sweet words of inspiration to go along, too! Thank you so much for lending an ear. You are very special.

Jill: Thank you for being the extra set of eyes that I needed for this project! You were thorough and patient. I appreciate your hard work and your input. Bless you, sweet friend.

And finally, Donna: Did you think I'd forgotten you? Through my temper tantrums, verb-tense issues, and long rambling emails—you've been there. In fact, you turned a passing remark in one of those emails into this book. Thank you for believing in me, and encouraging me. Thank you for suffering through my misuse of commas (I *swear* I passed English 101), my confused verb-tense, and my switching points of view! You've cleaned up after me, yet again, and produced something legible. Thank you, my friend.

Contents

· · · · · · · · · ·

Prologue

· · · · · · · · · · · ·

Well, I've run away from home. I knew eventually it would have to come to this. I'm sitting on a plane, cruising at a pleasant thirty-six thousand feet, skies are clear, the captain says we are right on target for an on-time landing in sunny San Diego, California. Who am I? Nobody, really. Just a mom. A tired mom...with three kids, a fairly demanding job, and a wonderfully sweet husband who knew I was about to crack— hence the plane ticket to Cali.

The idea for this book came to me a couple of weeks ago at about four thirty in the morning as I was cleaning up milk from a broken cup that my daughter had left on the kitchen table overnight. I'd stepped in the milk, barefooted, as I made my way half-asleep to the back door to let the dog out. Somehow, in the night, this seemingly indestructible cup that previously I was sure I could've backed over with my SUV and left intact had mysteriously split in two places down both sides by itself, thus spilling all of its contents. Milk—old milk—was everywhere. It was on the chair cushion (I assure you it smells lovely two weeks later), it was under the table—having used the grout on my kitchen floor as some type of superhighway to travel distances that I would've deemed impossible for milk to travel—and it was (naturally) all across my wooden table.

Why was the cup still sitting on the table overnight? you may be wondering.

My husband and I were trying a little experiment with our daughter, Emma. You see, she's eight years old. She's in the middle of two brothers—one older (he's nine), one younger (he's seven; you'll meet them both eventually)—and she suffers terribly from Princess Syndrome. She has this overwhelming feeling that everyone around her *must* wait on her. I've tried to convince her she's wrong. Those acts of extreme service are reserved for me. She refuses to clear her plate after meals, claiming to "forget." Jeff and I wanted to see how long she would allow dishes to remain at her place before she stopped "forgetting" and carried them to the sink. My brilliant plan backfired at four thirty in the morning of the first day, as I was on my hands and knees mopping up curdled milk from the night before.

Emma had won round one and she didn't even know it! Thus, *The Mommy Diaries: How I'm Surviving Parenting without Killing Anyone* was born.

Throughout the course of this book, I will introduce you to most of the members of my family, from the obvious (husband and kids), to the obscure (the in-laws and such). However, right now I'll cover the basics: My husband and I have three children altogether. In fact, we (and when I say *we*, I really mean *I*) had those children in twenty-six months.

I'll wait for a moment and let that one sink in for a minute... Three kids—twenty-six months—no multiple births. Let me warn you: this is not good for your body nor is it good for your mind. Both will come out slightly worse for wear by the time this is all said and done.

Please don't get me wrong, I love my children! I wouldn't trade them for anything...well, except this week...this week, I'm trading them all for some rest and relaxation in sunny San Diego with my sisters.

So please, sit back, grab a cup o' joe, and enjoy the trials and tribulations that are racing through my mind, as I offer you a bit of hope and encouragement (with some humor mixed in along the way), so that you, too, can *Survive Parenting without Killing Anyone*!

Ethan, Emma, & Elliott
Christmas, 2004

Dazed & Diapered

After a time of wandering around in portions of my newly lost mind, I am a firm believer that crazy people don't know they're crazy. They come to this realization much too late to do anything about it. For instance, had I known what the exact impact the words, "Honey, I want to have a baby," were really going to have on my marriage, my mind, my body, and just me in general...perhaps I would have waited longer to utter those famous last words of a fool.

It's always best to start at the beginning. That way, you don't leave anyone or anything out, and we all start this journey out on equal footing. Parenthood *can* be planned. In many various ways, one can decide when, where, and how to become a parent. In today's society, there are a multitude of paths parents-to-be can choose.

Option number one: Distance yourself from any and all traditional forms of birth control (i.e., pills, IUDs, condoms, and the like) and just let nature take its course.

Option two requires a little more planning on your part: You buy books that will instruct you as to how to chart body temperature, graphs by which to measure said body temperatures, then you must chart the time of day you took your temp...the whole nine yards. It's exhausting, but eventually it gets the job done.

Then you have option three: This is a bit more invasive, and requires the use of doctors, appointments, turkey basters, tools, and needles... I have a touch of "White Coat Syndrome," so talking about doctors and such tend to make me squirm.

Next, you move into option four: Adoption. This is one of the most intentional means of planning to parent that I know of. This process can take years and thousands of dollars. But in the end, you have a child that you have all but hand-picked.

Intentional parenting. In all of these forms, we have to be *intentional* through *all* of our parenting. Through every step and phase of these various forms of acquiring the babies, we read books, talk to people, and of course—watch TV. We build up in our minds the way we think having babies and raising kids is supposed to happen. We do this with the hope of trying to better prepare ourselves for the task at hand...and that task is, *What in the world we are going to do with these perfect little angels once we invite them into our hearts and bring them into our homes?* Having lived through this initial stage of preparation three times, might I make a suggestion to any first-time-trying-to-be-mommies out there?—RUN! LOCK THE DOOR AND RUN!

You see, I wanted to be a mother from a very young age. In fact, it was all I could ever really remember wanting to be when I grew up. I dabbled with thoughts of becoming a teacher or a nurse...but the nurse thing went out the door when I discovered I would have to deal with actual body fluids. And teachers are probably some of the most under-paid and under-appreciated people on the face of the entire planet. So, I reverted back to my original plan, which was to marry the man of my dreams and raise the picture-perfect family that you find on TV, in movies, and on the cover of magazines like *Good Housekeeping* and *Family Circle*. Had I known back then just how closely my family would actually resemble a circle, or even a *circus*, maybe I would've suffered through nursing school and followed through with the whole nursing thing!

I am the oldest of four girls, and there is quite an age gap (eight, ten, and twelve years-to be exact) between myself and my three sisters, so I had the opportunity to play "babies" when each one of my sisters was born. I dressed them up. I put them in makeshift baby beds. I watched them roll off of my bed and onto the floor. (Sorry Mother, now you know what's wrong with a couple of them! They must've hit the floor one too many times!) I was a built-in babysitter for my parents, and that was okay with me. I enjoyed it. I was good at it...well, except for dropping them—but that was only a couple of times.

The main difference between babysitting my sisters and caring for my own children is that, with my sisters, I could always hand them back to my mother when they proved to be more of a handful than I had hands to shift to. When you have children of your own, there isn't anyone to tag-team with. You are it. Always. However, that thought didn't really occur to me until much too late to do anything about it...like when the hospital sent me home with my first child. But we'll talk more about that in a bit.

This book is about how I survived once I acted upon those urges to fulfill the most basic need to procreate. I'm going to share with you what happened in my world once we brought three kids home in a time span that is barely long enough to build a house, let alone build multiple kids! My prayer is that you find comfort in knowing that you are not the only one suffering from Post-Traumatic Stress Disorder or Buyer's Remorse. And yes, it's okay to admit that *both* of those conditions apply to parenting; though hopefully, not all the time. Parenting truly is one of the most rewarding experiences of your life, and, when done right, it will also be one of the most heartbreaking. Our children need us to be more than friends, more than fun, more than cool. They need us to be their parents.

Jeff and I had been married about six months when I announced one day that I thought we needed to start "trying." In all of his male wisdom, he simply stared back at me and said, "Trying to do what?" Duh. I explained that I was ready to have a baby. Being a fairly well-educated man, he knew what was involved in getting pregnant; therefore he was 100 percent on board with the process of *trying*. After all, everyone we knew was having trouble getting pregnant. We had no idea what we were in for. It took us two months. Come to find out, *getting* pregnant was not going to be the problem with us... *Not getting* me pregnant turned out to be the bigger challenge. But again, that's for later.

When I saw two pink lines on the home pregnancy test, I slid down the bathroom wall...literally...and left a huge black mark on the cream-colored wall. I had been wearing black jeans. Jeff had to repaint. I rushed out and bought every book under the sun. I was going to fully educate myself on what was going on inside my body. I took high school biology and health class, but suddenly that seemed like a really long time ago, and I wanted to know for sure about the day-by-day changes that were happening. Those books didn't really do much except scare the life out of me with all of the warnings and horror stories about the .0045 percent chance that my baby was going to be born as his own sister because of the fact that I'd eaten sushi the week before I knew I was pregnant. Couple that with all of the medication I was taking due to extreme nausea, and *voila*! He was also going to be armless and legless if he managed to arrive at all.

I also bought my loving husband books on how to love your wife through her pregnancy, how to be a first-time daddy, and of course, every first-time parent's Bibles: *What to Expect When You're Expecting* and *What to Expect the First Year*. I'm not sure those books were ever opened by anyone except me, and that may have been when I bought them. I will say, though, they make excellent doorstops on blustery days in Houston, Texas, when both the front and the back doors of the house are open, and the wind has a tendency to want to slam both doors shut! I found out rather quickly that not all men found the miracle of growing a life inside you, well, all that miraculous. The "glow" that you hear about isn't anything more than the sweat that glistens on your forehead after you've thrown up for the forty-second time that day. I had the "glow" for twenty-six months straight. You could've used me for a night light.

When I got pregnant with my first child, I was thrilled. When you are pregnant with your first baby, you have all of these grand visions of how your life is going to be. You have even stronger visions and convictions about all of the millions of things you are NOT going to do with your child. You almost keep a running tally of the scores of mistakes that your friends are making with their little spawns in your purse, because you know full well that you can do better. Your child will *not* act that way in public. And let's face it, with a baby in the belly and none to chase at home...life is good. Hormones make you delusional. You have the time to obsess over how perfect Junior is going to be when he effortlessly pops out into the world and you are back in your pre-pregnancy jeans in two weeks. Two words: Dream on.

I'm here to tell you all of the things that your friends won't tell you, and the other books are too scared to. Your favorite soap opera lies to you. You know those wonderfully beautiful women with perfectly round baby-bumps? Very seldom does that happen in real life; occasionally, but rarely. Those women: (a) are not pregnant, (b) have spent *hours* in makeup because ratings would drop significantly if the producers actually put a woman on the air with the real pregnancy "glow," and (c) stay pregnant for eighteen months with their brother's baby and then deliver a preemie. Do you really want that kind of life? I don't think so.

Coming back to reality, your boobs will swell to the size of county fair watermelons *while* you are pregnant. No joke. Your husband will think he's died and gone to heaven until he finds out that he cannot touch them because anything that swells that much and that fast will hurt. *After* delivery, call

The Guinness Book of World Records. With my first baby, I went from a pre-pregnancy B cup to an after-baby EE cup. No joke. I thought Jeff's eyes were going to pop out of his head. I needed a cane in order to walk upright.

These days, hospitals will only keep you long enough to make sure you get the right kid from the delivery room. Even with all of my babysitting (which totally doesn't prepare you for mothering your own), I was terrified to be sent home with our firstborn, Ethan. I'm not a big crier. However, I cried when I was told to leave the hospital. "You just CAN'T send me home with him! What am I going to do?!" The nurses who heard my cries assured me that Jeff and I would do just fine. I didn't think they were right. Three days later, I proved them wrong. I mentioned that I grew up with sisters. As it turns out, God has a wonderful sense of humor, thus making my first child a *boy*. As you may know, boys come packaged a little bit differently than girls... In fact, boys come packaged A LOT differently than girls. They have an added appendage. Come to find out, these extra appendages need extra care.

We had Ethan circumcised in the hospital by our pediatrician before we were released. She came in and told us all about the care and cleaning that we were going to have to maintain from home. I got very lightheaded. Jeff got very pale. I'm not sure this method is still practiced. Anyway, Ethan had a ring placed around the tip of his penis to keep the incision nice and neat and trim looking. Within X number of days, it (the ring, not the penis) would simply fall off. We just needed to keep Neosporin on it and all would be good. Sounds easy, right? Wrong.

The trouble started when I realized that babies don't sleep.

Well, they probably sleep more than their parents. It's just that they are very noisy sleepers. They make all sorts of grunts and groans which lead new parents (check that: new *mommies*) to believe that they are awake and they must be hungry or wet or, at the very least, they (the babies) need to be tended to right away. I found myself in this predicament one night. Ethan was hovering somewhere around a week old. I don't think I'd slept since he was born. I now had sandpaper on the inside of my eyelids every time I tried to blink or shut them. It's an awesome feeling. He made a noise; I got up. I changed his diaper. I nursed him from one side...which by the way, in the beginning, feels as though you have stuck your breast through a meat grinder that is on the slowest possible speed with the dullest possible blade. I highly recommend it. He finished. I was crying. My toes were slowly starting to uncurl. I got up from the rocker and walked to the changing table because every time this kid ate, he pooped. It was amazing. Here's where the fun begins.

Ethan hated having his diaper changed. He would kick. He would cry. He would kick some more. He would pee all over me. This was the night that my reflexes were not as fast as they should've been because as he kicked, I moved the diaper and his heel caught the edge of the diaper, which somehow managed to hook the edge of the circumcision ring—which—pulled—it—halfway—off. I screamed. Ethan screamed. Jeff almost had a heart attack.

Here's the deal, every night since we had brought Ethan home, Jeff had slept through all of the feedings and the diaper changes, greeting me each morning with, "How'd the baby do last night?" This was one night he couldn't ignore. I was hysterical. I was screaming, "I BROKE HIM! I BROKE HIM!" Ethan was screaming. Jeff was delirious. It seems I'd truly awakened him up from a dead sleep, which is amazing to me—even now. We had to take the ring off. Well, Jeff had to take the ring off. I couldn't do it. It was awful. He did it, though. Ethan survived. Amazingly enough, he's still intact. We did, in fact, make it through the night. I nursed him back to sleep...I didn't sleep for another three years. Sleep is overrated.

I prayed for a girl the next time around.

I'm thankful Ethan was a record-holding nurser. The kid could eat! So, all of my overabundance wasn't wasted. I never really was one of those parents to follow all of the rules about feeding only every two hours or four hours or whenever the "experts" said to feed. I'm not sure the experts have ever held a baby, let alone have children of their own. I didn't really ever know how much milk Ethan was getting, it's not like you develop ounce marks on your breast after delivery— although, strategically placed stretch marks could help. The bottom line was: When he seemed hungry, I fed him. I found out with Ethan that I could do a lot of things one-handed that I previously thought required two hands. I can eat with one hand. I can make lunch with one hand. If the need was really great—in an emergency situation—I can even go to the bathroom with one hand. The kid *loved* to eat. I was his favorite meal ticket and/or pacifier, which made it all the more strange when, at about five months old, he quit nursing cold-turkey. This phenomenon kind of freaked me out a little. I wasn't quite sure what to make of it. I didn't give it a whole lot of thought, though. I mean he *was* growing...maybe he was just hungry...well, hungri*er*. He *had* been eyeing the mashed potatoes around the dinner table lately. I was a little disappointed he wasn't into the whole nursing thing anymore, but I managed to move on.

As I told you, he was our first baby, and I had plans. Big plans. His little life was all laid out. I was going to nurse him for a year…or so I thought. That was what was best for him… *everyone* said so. I enjoyed the bonding time it afforded us. It was our time together. About six weeks after he decided I wasn't exactly fitting his taste anymore, I realized that my monthly visits from Aunt Flo had not returned to normal. In fact, they hadn't returned at all. I wasn't thoroughly concerned. My doctor had told me that it would take some time for my body to readjust to not being pregnant, and to no longer be breastfeeding. I was supposed to wait and be patient. However, two weeks later: still nothing. I began to get a little concerned. I called my doctor again. He advised me to take a home pregnancy test. My immediate thought was, *Why?* I'd just had a baby, and I just finished nursing that baby, there was no way that I could be pregnant.

I was wrong.

Apparently not being able to get pregnant while breastfeeding is an old wives' tale. You *can* conceive while nursing. Here's the kicker: Ethan knew it. The influx of hormones into my system due to the conception of his impending little sister changed the flavor of his food supply. That's why he quit nursing cold-turkey. He didn't like it anymore. Can you say guilt, party of one? So, we're going to have another baby. Super. They are going to be close. Really close. Really, *really* close. Ethan will turn one in August; baby number two is due in October. You do the math.

When Jeff and I celebrated our first wedding anniversary, I was pregnant with Ethan. When we celebrated our second wedding anniversary I was pregnant with Emma...I just hadn't figured that out yet. Having only dated for seven months before getting married, the fact of the matter is: At this point in our relationship, he has known me pregnant longer than he has known me not pregnant. Awesome. Thankfully, he doesn't spook easily. I'm not exactly what you'd call a "peach" while pregnant. Don't worry, I don't throw knives or spit fire...I just don't handle pregnancy very well. I can *get* pregnant—no problem. I'm just among the sickest on the planet while incubating those sweet little honey buns. The sicker I get, the more dehydrated I get; the more dehydrated I get, the more often I have to make a run to the hospital for fluids. It's a fantastic cycle. That bumps me right up into the high-risk category. Remember the "glow"? I had it all the time. But there are lots of games you can play with your infant son from the couch or the bathroom floor that he will find highly amusing. For instance: Toss a couch cushion across the room and have him go get it. Babies love that! Mommy gets to lay still. Goldfish crackers...yummy snack for him/super absorbent tummy soother for you. Ginger-based, sugar-free lollipops... (sometimes) useful aid for mom/healthy treat for him.

Jeff and I didn't have any family that lived near us in the early years of our marriage. That was a bit of challenge while I was going through the difficulties of my pregnancy with Emma. Thankfully, I had a really good nanny to help with childcare for Ethan or I simply would not have made it! My parents lived in Austin at the time, (a solid, two-and-a-half-hour drive away) and they were still occupied with their own parenting of my little sisters who still lived at home—plus, they owned two restaurants that kept them pretty busy.

My in-laws all lived out-of-state. My mother-in-law lived just outside of Chicago, but, with the arrival of Ethan, she found it more and more difficult to stay away from us, and when I say "us," I mean Ethan. To prove that point, she would fly in about every four to six weeks. One afternoon, my mother-in-law, Carol—who eventually just changed her name to Nana—flew into town from Chicago for a visit. Ever since the arrival of her first-born grandson, the sun no longer rises in the East and sets in the West. Nope, now it rose over Ethan's crib, and set wherever he happened to be. This particular visit fell about six months into this second pregnancy, which was around the same time that the concrete realization hit me that I was indeed having another baby.

Another stunning realization was the difference between Braxton Hicks (false labor) contractions and the real deal...I'd had my fair share of Braxton Hicks contractions with Ethan, so I wasn't overly concerned with this round until I got stuck in traffic on my way to the airport to pick up Carol, and actually had the time to start timing them. Sweet. They were ten minutes apart. I live in Houston, so sitting in traffic is an excellent place to go into preterm labor. I mean, if I had to deliver this kid in my truck, she would have been in middle school before the traffic jam cleared out. This wasn't exactly ideal.

I called my doctor just to let him know what I thought was going on. He was more than a little put out with me that I was refusing to alter my present course and head to the hospital (by this time, I promised him the traffic flow was moving). I told him that I just had to grab my mother-in-law and I would meet him at the hospital. No big deal, right? Wrong again. Only trouble with this plan was that, by the time I got to the airport, my contractions were seven minutes apart and getting slightly stronger. Maybe this wasn't such a great idea. But, I should get extra points for almost making my mother-in-law faint. I waddled out of my SUV, told her I was very sorry, but that I couldn't help her with her bags because I thought I was in labor, so she really needed to hurry. I swear, I thought she was a goner!

Once we made it to the hospital, even *I* was getting a little nervous. We had called Jeff; he was en route from two hours away and probably breaking land speed records to get to me. Carol was practicing my Lamaze breathing for me. I was still driving. (I have control issues...) However, I didn't park my own truck. I let her do it; thankfully, I had enough sense left in me to know that hauling my pregnant self all the way through the parking garage wasn't the best idea.

Contractions: five minutes and counting. Time to panic.

It was too early for this baby to come. Six and a half months is not exactly a prime delivery date. Three minutes. With the IV inserted, meds started flowing, heart started racing...contractions stopped. This baby girl (wouldn't you know it'd be a girl...shrouded in drama) was trying very hard to make her appearance early. I was already dilating, effacing... the whole nine yards. My doctor was furious with me. You have to understand something: Dr. Wilson is the kindest and most understanding man I know to go through pregnancies with...well, for being a man, and never actually having had the opportunity to *be* pregnant. However, on this particular day, "kind and understanding" were not exactly the words I would have used.

"You already weren't feeling well? You *still* went to the airport? You *waited* to come here?... Bed rest."

He may have well just broken my legs. I hate being still. I hate being *told* to be still. And what was worse, I had a witness...my mother-in-law was standing right there beside me, and promised to be my warden while she was in town. She stayed an extra week.

Turns out, Emma (that's what we named the baby) was just a little impatient. She liked to do things her way. She still does. (Hence the milk and the plates on the table...don't even get me started on her room.) She did end up staying put until fairly close to her due date, although we seriously thought she was going to make her appearance at home, and now looking back—that was probably my fault. Note to self: Do not ingest castor oil unless you feel like inducing hard labor and are prepared to play catch with your newborn. I mean, I *knew* castor oil brought on labor. I just didn't know how *fast*...

In my defense, I was sort of done with being pregnant. Remember, I'd been pregnant for a couple of years now, and someone had mentioned that castor oil would sort of speed the pregnancy process along. They were right. But what they failed to mention was how speedy it would become.

Start to finish, Emma was born in two and a half hours. That's from the very first contraction to the final push. Jeff was so excited! He got to drive like Mario Andretti all the way to the hospital. I was somewhat concerned he was going to have to morph from Mario to McSteamy if he had to deliver his daughter in the front seat of my truck. Thankfully, we did make it to the hospital on time...barely. Might I take this time to offer you ladies out there who are thinking that maybe you'd like to go the natural delivery route... TAKE THE DRUGS! Girls, I've had three kids: two with meds, one without. Take the drugs as soon as they are offered. Your anesthesiologist will become your very best friend. You will love him more and more with every push of the magic button. Trust me. Needless to say, with Emma—no drugs.

Delivering a baby with no drugs is the weirdest feeling in the world. It's not magical. It's not enlightening. It didn't make me more of a real woman. I simply did not have time to get them. The best time for an epidural is right after you find out you're pregnant. I did feel better, though, after her delivery, in the sense that I could get up and walk around. But the *during* part was rough.

Dazed and diapered. That was us. I had two itty-bitty ones at home. Happy, healthy kiddos...a boy and girl: a matched set. Life was good. And we were done. My mother-in-law was visiting...seemed a bit longer this time than the last time, but I needed the extra hands. I was adjusting to no sleep. Jeff was becoming a hands-on dad. He didn't seem quite so afraid to pick up this second baby as he was with the first one. Whenever Ethan, as a newborn or an infant, would cry, Jeff would pick him up (at my insistence) and hold him at arm's length, as though the kid were a bomb and might explode at any given minute. Over the course of the last year with Ethan, Jeff had some time to adjust to the fact that babies cry, and rarely do they explode—so holding them close to your body was not only a safe bet, but a good call, as this, in most cases, would quiet their cries. We were also talking about him going to see that "special" doctor. We had all we could handle with these two babies. We didn't need any more. We were doing okay. Or so we thought...

There comes a time in everyone's life, a pivotal moment where you have an opportunity to make a choice. I will forever remember our moment in time. Jeff went through a period where he traveled quite a bit for work. He would be gone anywhere from four to six days a week, two to three weeks a month. It was a bit hectic with two babies at the house when he was gone. The kids were little—in fact, Emma was barely six weeks old, Jeff's mother was still visiting (although at this point, we thought she'd moved in, without really telling us) so it was a rare moment that our house was ever completely empty. Jeff was leaving to go on a weeklong business trip and his mom had taken the kids to the nanny, so the two of us were *alone*. Well, as we said our goodbyes, one thing lead to another...and a quick kiss goodbye turned into a long kiss goodbye, and he went away for his weeklong trip feeling very satisfied. I went through the rest of my day with a bit more spring in my step as well.

Life returned to normal, Jeff's mom told us she was moving in, Ethan was adjusting to Emma, Emma was adjusting to life on the outside, I was adjusting to life with two babies, Jeff made his appointment with his "special" doctor...then Emma quit nursing.

I almost fainted.

I could not bring myself to go to the store and buy the test. I called my friend, Ann. She bought a two-pack with a bonus stick. I took one immediately. Positive. I drank some water, and then took the second test. *More* positive.

I sat down in the middle of my bathroom and cried. I took the third test the next morning. Super positive...first morning urine... I had to tell my husband. I mean, I couldn't exactly keep this from him. It was also the morning of his *appointment*. I laid all three tests on his counter in the bathroom. He turned as white as a ghost and dropped into the chair that I sit in to put on my make-up. He just sat there shaking his head.

I said, "I know. Get dressed. I'm driving."

· · · · · ·

The "special" doctor was an enlightening experience for the both of us. Jeff had gotten used to going to the doctor with me, and he was familiar with watching me have to go through the absolute mortification of disrobing, trying to cover myself with something slightly larger than a BBQ napkin, climb onto a table and wait (for an eternity) for the doctor to come in. His appointment was a different story. The man mumbled, and groaned, and complained, and mumbled some more with every piece of clothing he took off.

He unhooked his belt: "This is ridiculous."

He untucked his shirt: "It's cold in here."

He unbuttoned his pants: "Are you (looking at me) going to watch?"

He mumbled something colorful when he discovered he'd forgotten to remove his shoes before trying to remove his pants.

He climbed onto the table.

He tried (unsuccessfully) to position the napkin to effectively cover himself: "This stupid thing is too small! It doesn't fit!"

He fidgeted: "How long do I have to sit here—"

In came the doctor.

Dr. Snippet: "Good morning, Mr. Louis. How are you this morning?"

Jeff: "Fine."

Dr. Snippet: "That's great." He looked at his chart. "I see we're here today for a vasectomy. Are you sure?" The doctor turned to look at me.

Jeff: Through gritted teeth and no smile: "Pretty sure. She told me this morning, she's pregnant—again."

Dr. Snippet: "Wonderful! Congratulations! How many will this make?"

Me: "This is number three. Our son is one, our daughter is eight weeks old... Please do a good job."

Dr. Snippet: "Wow. Let's get started. Now, Mr. Louis, if you could just lay back and put your feet in the stirrups, so I can have a look..."

I smiled. Jeff had a whole new appreciation for my doctor visits after his visit to Dr. Snippet. Isn't life funny?

Jeff did survive his appointment. You know the stereotype about everyone in Texas riding a horse to and from work? Well, for the next couple of days, we couldn't have convinced any out-of-towners of anything contrary by the way Jeff was walking! Poor thing! But, he managed to pull through it, and return to his normal activities within no time at all. As for me...well, I wasn't fairing quite so well. Baby number three was proving to be a bit more difficult than one and two *combined*.

I'm not a very big person. My driver's license says I'm five foot three inches, but I think they measured me with my Big

Girl Shoes on. I don't weigh much over one hundred pounds, even with the heavily magnified boobs I was carrying around. So, as my pregnancy with this baby progressed, so did the bouts of nausea. Extreme nausea. *Champion* nausea. I lost fifteen pounds, which, needless to say, landed me back in the hospital—only this time I wasn't privy to a couple of bags of fluid and a pat on the head to drink my water and go home. No, no. This time, I landed myself a sweet little vacation at a happening resort known as St. Luke's Medical Center on the north side.

If Elliott (which is what we named the baby) had been my first baby, he would've been an only child. At this point in my marriage—check that—in my *whole relationship with my husband*, he's known me longer pregnant than not pregnant. Crazy. And speaking of crazy...that's what hormones tend to do to you. Women, at any given moment in time, have raging hormones that cause us to behave in ways that are outside the patterns of normal society. But, when that same woman is pregnant, look out!—because she now has a chemical world-war raging inside her that she has absolutely no control over. Every time (there were more than a couple times) I landed myself in the hospital, it was for a time period of no less than one week. This made parenting two babies left at home exceedingly challenging. I'm thankful my mother-in-law was there to pick up the slack that I couldn't even look at, let alone carry.

This pregnancy proved to be a bit more than Jeff could handle as well. He was traveling and still working at the office when he was in town, and now, with having to make regular trips out to St. Luke's to visit me, needless to say, this added a large dose of stress to our marriage. Let me tell you something girls: It's perfectly okay to be frustrated with your husband. Jeff was plenty frustrated with me. Although I don't see how I could've changed the situation. I don't handle being still very well. But seeing as how I was hooked up to several different monitors and machines, walking around was difficult and leaving the hospital was highly improbable. Therefore, Jeff had to come and see me. Have you ever found yourself in a situation where you knew it would be better if you could just remain quiet and not say anything? But instead of choosing to do the right thing, you detour down a really wrong path and all sorts of things begin to fly from your wide-open trap? That's where I found myself one night.

Jeff had come in for a "visit," although on this particular night it felt like a pity visit or an I-have-to-be-here-because-you're-my-wife visit. At any rate, I wasn't thrilled to see him, nor was he thrilled to be there. Bottom line: words were said on both sides that should not have been said; I'm certain that the nurses enjoyed the scene. In retrospect, "scene" may not be the right word…"Broadway musical" may fit a bit more accurately. I ended up telling him that I didn't need or want his sympathy and if this was how he was going to act…he could just stay away. He didn't say another word to me. He turned and walked out. I was numb. Every marriage, every *relationship*, goes through times like this one. Daily stress gets the better of you.

See, Jeff was dealing with being Mommy and Daddy, along with running his business, and making sure his mother was okay (remember she was living with us), along with worrying about me and the baby I was carrying. That's an awful lot for a man to have lug around with him. In my defense,

I couldn't care for the babies I'd left at home because every time I took two steps I threw up. I was exhausted, dehydrated, and starving. At this point, I'd been stuck in a hospital bed for longer than I cared to remember, and if my doctor didn't do something brilliant, I was going to be in this same hospital bed until I delivered this baby! Mix all of that with some high-grade hormonal weapons of mass destruction and you have an explosion of astronomical proportions just waiting to happen. Jeff and I were having a hard time remembering how I got pregnant in the first place.

Turns out, my doctor did do something brilliant. He installed a diabetic pump into me. No, I'm not diabetic, but this pump followed the same regime for administration of medication that it would have for a diabetic on insulin. In short, this pump was my ticket out of St. Luke's and gave me the opportunity to go home. It didn't fix me completely, but it did allow me the chance to be around my babies on a more regular basis. I still couldn't completely care for them, as I was still violently ill, but I could hold them and love on them.

My living room is a lot closer than my hospital room. Jeff and I made up as well. We both realized that tensions were running a little high. Being married isn't the most difficult thing you have to do in life...it's throwing kids into that mix. Aside from being sicker than a dog for the entire nine months, I delivered a healthy, seven-pound baby boy just three weeks early. During my pregnancy with Elliott, I was one of those women with the perfectly round baby bump...but not by choice...and not for lack of trying. I simply could not keep anything down. I lost a total of fifteen pounds with him, and then gained ten of them back.

October, 2003 Ethan resting on my belly,
feeling his new little brother moving around!

This child has a plan and a purpose. He is my walking,
talking miracle.

Through the sleep-deprived fog that had enveloped my
brain...I remembered the whole circumcision ring debacle, so
I was much more careful this time around. Elliott survived the
first two weeks of his life with almost no mishaps. Almost.
We did bring him home to a one-year-old (barely) sister and
a two-year-old brother. Their idea of a welcome to the family
gift? Emma threw the television remote at him within hours
of our arrival. Apparently she wanted a sister. She still stands
by that request today. I have assured her that we cannot return
her little brother in the same way that he was delivered to us.
She remains, eight years later, miffed.

So, for those of you who may be wandering around in

your own newly discovered portions of an abandoned brain, let me bring you up to speed: at this point in time, I am now the proud parent of a zero-year-old, one-year-old, and two-year-old. Ethan had turned two in August, Emma turned one in October, and just eight days after Emma's first birthday, I delivered Elliott. People asked if Jeff and I owned a TV. We said that we did...two, in fact. The next question that usually followed as they gawked at all these babies was, "Do you ever turn them on?" Haha. Very funny. We do now. It's the only way we get any rest. I'm telling you, Dora is truly a great explorer. And Bob the Builder can build anything he wants to as long as he builds the attention span of my children long enough for me to shower and shave *both* legs in the same day.

It was during the early weeks after the arrival of Elliott that I began to feel overwhelmed. I know what you're thinking. *Now* she feels overwhelmed? You see, my mother-in-law decided that it was time to find a job, Jeff was still traveling, and that left me at home...alone...with three kids—actually three babies. I developed a drooling problem that was almost as fantastic as my daughter's. Elliott decided that screaming was way better than crying. Just for the record: There is a difference between a crying kid and a screaming kid. The only thing that remotely made Elliott stop the insanely deafening sounds that came from his tiny body was me—being used as a pacifier.

It was during one of those times of trying to calm the beast within his little self that mass chaos broke out in my house. I had just positioned myself on the couch, shoved his favorite "binky" into his mouth, took one deep, calming breath—when I heard the sound of glass shattering from the kitchen.

Kids are so smart. Can you appreciate how smart they

are? Ethan and Emma knew that when I assumed the position, supported (and pinned in, from their point of view)
by all of the needed pillows to maintain my proper feeding
stance that I was effectively deemed "out of commission" and
could no longer move at lightning speed. They were wrong. As
I said, I had just settled Elliott down when I heard glass break
behind me. I immediately removed Elliott from me (which
launched him into new fits of hysteria) and vaulted over the
back of the couch to find Ethan and Emma standing on top of
the kitchen table staring down at the shattered pieces of a red
vase that held the remains of flowers that should have been
thrown out long before that day. But, this particular point in
time was not the time to dwell on that fact. I perfected my
Spider-Man skills by jumping from chair to barstool to chair,
all the while screaming at the kids (over the top of Elliott's
ear-splitting cries), "DON'T MOVE! STAY WHERE YOU ARE!
ETHAN, WHAT DID YOU DO?! WHY DID YOU LET YOUR
SISTER ON THE TABLE?!"

Let's stop right here for a minute. Ethan is two. His
deranged mother is climbing from all the chairs in the kitchen
in some wild attempt to get to the top of the table before the
kids try and escape, all the while being serenaded by the wails
of a screaming infant. The blank look of solid confusion radi-
ating from Ethan's face should've been a clue to me; however,
rational thought had left the building. Rational thought may
have been gone, but Monster Mom was here in full force. Still
ranting. Still charging. Still grappling over furniture, dangling
over broken glass, fully expecting my two-year-old son to
explain in a coherent manner the whys and hows behind the
broken vase. It didn't happen. Instead, I grabbed both babies
in sort of a football hold and went out the kitchen in a differ-

ent route, as to avoid the river of broken glass, and banished them to the safety of the upstairs.

I resumed my seat on the couch with Elliott and attempted to calm him down. You'd think, having nursed all these kids for as long as I'd been doing it, that my breasts would not have hurt as bad as they did. Totally not true. So, as Ethan and Emma were upstairs crying, Elliott would suck, and then cry...and I sat on the couch sobbing about the lot I'd somehow gotten saddled with. The best part—there was still glass to clean up when I was done with the baby. Dazed and diapered. Awesome.

I did get the glass cleaned up. Elliott did not stop crying for the remainder of the day. The other two, however, did keep a wide berth around me. By the end of the day, I was a complete catastrophe. My nerves were shot. I'd held Elliott all day long. Ethan wanted a cup of milk or juice or something, but at that particular point in my day, he may as well have asked me for the moon. Emma happened to follow him into the kitchen, where she, too, thought she was thirsty. It's very difficult to twist the lid onto a belligerent sippy cup while holding a squirming infant in your other hand. With all of the events that had led up to this request...an uncooperative cup was more than I could bear. I'm amazed I managed to get the lid on, but when I finally did...I took the cup and threw it. I sat down in the middle of the kitchen floor and cried. Ethan took his little sister by the hand, and took her away from me.

I want to take another opportunity to offer anyone out there who is reading this a lifeline. I made a phone call while sitting in a puddle of my own tears and self-pity to a friend—my best friend. She came to my rescue (and that of the kids) and took them to her house for a while. Did you know that losing one hour (of the recommended eight hours nightly) of sleep for six consecutive nights will have the same effect on your body as pulling an all-nighter? That's just for one week. I didn't know this at the time of my Nolan Ryan attempted strike-out, but just think about all the sleep I'd lost over the past *two years*. I basically could've been awake for about one hundred days...give or take a few here and there. With that type of sleep deprivation, coupled with the hormone world war raging inside me...no wonder I was trying to pitch a no-hitter!

I began to think that I might need some pharmaceutical intervention. Incidentally, this was also the night that I pulled Jeff out of bed around two thirty by one of his favorite appendages so he could merely sit at my feet and simply be close enough for me to reach, while I nursed *his* baby for the forty-seventh time that day. I was tired. I was tired of being the only one who could feed the baby; tired of being the only one who could hear the other two cry in the night. I slept (and I use that word loosely) with *two* baby monitors beside my bed. I had to write the kids' names on them, so I would know whose room to go to. I was flat-out exhausted. The next morning, I called my doctor.

He listened to me cry. He listened to me scream. He listened to me cry some more. Then he prescribed a miracle pill that made me not want to throw knives at my husband or sippy cups through the walls. I was able to adjust, breathe, and deal with having three babies at home. I found my rhythm. Taking this little pill every day did not mean that I was somehow a failure as a wife and mother. No. In fact, to me, it meant the opposite. I recognized that I could not do this on my own. I also recognized that Jeff could not read my mind. When I need his help, I have to ask for it. By the way, that is still true today. I was also thankful that I had a friend I could call when things got ugly. Parenting is not for sissies. These sweet little angels will test you in the most brutal ways. You will doubt everything you've ever believed to be true about yourself and what you thought you'd do in any given situation.

Is it worth it?

Absolutely. Without one single, solitary doubt.

But, just as you'd never go hiking or camping without proper provisions, never attempt to parent without proper provisions as well. Dazed and diapered. I am glad that phase is over. But without it, I never would've understood why some animals eat their young...

Orlando, 2006

The first day of our first encounter with Disney World!

Why Some Animals
Eat Their Young

L et me ask you something. Have you ever planned a family vacation? Or maybe you're not at that actual stage of parenting yet... Maybe you're still in the "planning to plan a family vacation" phase. Want some advice? Stay in the planning phase for a while longer. You see, a couple of years ago, I planned a family vacation to the mother of all destinations: Walt Disney World in Orlando, Florida. Apparently, I was temporarily insane. For an added bonus, I decided we would go over Spring Break. The fact that it was Spring Break didn't really mean a hill of beans to me; my kids were small enough not to have to worry with that. However, my thirteen-year-old babysitter could only go with us over Spring Break, so I made some adjustments to our time. At the time of our departure from the Houston airport, my children's ages were two, three and four years old. I'll pause right there for the gasp. Oh, did

I mention that my husband was *meeting* us in Florida? He had scheduled something of mondo importance that simply could not wait...and 747's don't wait either. So, I boarded my Continental flight bound for the "Happiest Place on Earth" with my two-year-old, my three-year-old, my four-year-old and a bewildered-looking thirteen-year-old sitter, who wasn't quite sure she was feeling up to the task of accompanying me to Disney World.

I could feel the passengers' eyes boring into me as we passed them, while they offered up their silent prayers of, *Please God, don't let that group be sitting next to me.* Thankfully, Florida isn't that far from Houston, and the kids did amazingly well...considering. Let me just say, portable DVD players are a gift straight from God, and individual packets of snacks came down in the same miraculous gift bag. I went through my entire bag of tricks on that flight, but the kids were quiet, they stayed in their seats, and no one came up to me offering to stow an unruly child in the overhead bin for me. I considered the trip to Florida a win.

The airport in Orlando was another story. I have no scientific evidence to support this, but I believe that children (of any age) only have a certain amount of "good points" on any given day. That particular day, my kids burned every one of them on the plane ride to Florida. They had me believing that the angelic faces they were displaying for all the world to see were actually going to be the characteristics they were going to exhibit for the duration of the day. I was wrong. As soon as we were released from the plane and began making our way through the walkway from the plane to the airport, I started noticing the change taking place inside them. Elliott was two, so he was on my hip as I waited for the luggage guys to bring up the stroller from the belly of the plane. Ethan and Emma, however, were free from restraint…and they bolted. What they didn't know was that my sitter was a track star. She caught both of them and wrangled them back to where I was strapping Elliott into the stroller. I swear, with just one glimpse into Ethan's eyes, I could see the wheels of his little mind turning, planning his next escape. Jasmine (fitting that our sitter's name was Jasmine and we were headed to Disney World, where we might actually run into the *real* Jasmine) had a good grip on Ethan and Emma's hands as we made our way into the airport. The walk was slow as we were burdened with diaper bags that had once been neatly packed, but that had now been completely ransacked during the flight in the attempt to keep the kids calm and quiet.

Ethan then decided he didn't want to hold Jasmine's hand any longer; he wanted mine. Okay, here I was, pushing the stroller, holding bags, trying not to run over anyone—what's one more thing to hold on to? I could see the whole thing playing out in slow motion. As I reached for Ethan's hand, he looked up at me with his incredible big blue eyes and his round cherub cheeks, flashed a perfectly mischievous grin… and took off. Snap. "Go get him," I told Jasmine. Emma just stood there laughing and saying, "Ethan fast!" *Yes*, I thought. *Ethan is fast. But Mom has a plan. Time for extreme measures.*

There are certain truths in life one must adhere to. Always wear clean underwear in case you're in an accident. Always eat your vegetables, so you can grow to be big and strong. And my absolute favorite: Never say never; it will always come back to bite you. There were so many "nevers" in my vocabulary before I had children… Y'all, I could write another book just off of those! This "never" deals with leashes. I used to see parents with their kids on leashes, and think to my brilliant, child-less self, *What's wrong with* **those** *parents? Can't they control their small child? I'll* **never** *put* **my** *child on a leash!* Well, after Ethan's second attempt at freedom, it was time for the puppy backpacks...a.k.a.:leashes. For those of you who don't know what I'm talking about, allow me to explain: These backpacks are soft and fluffy stuffed animals. Kids love them. They can hold them. They can love on them. They can even put a few (very few) toys in the pouch of these backpacks. They go on like regular backpacks, but they clip across your child's chest, so said child cannot wiggle out of it. They come in a couple of different varieties: puppy, monkey, frog, and some other animal that no one really knows what it is. Parents love these backpacks because of their six-foot-long tail. Yes, it's all cute and fuzzy, but let's call a spade, a spade. Folks, this backpack is a *leash*. And I bought three of them.

As Jasmine made her way through the crowd to us with a laughing Ethan on her back, I had to re-group. I had made a very big deal about how special these backpacks were, and that we couldn't use them until we got to Florida. The kids had no idea they were to be used as a supplemental restraint system. I smiled the same smile Ethan had given me before he ran off, and asked him if he wanted his very special backpack. Of course he did! So did Emma. And naturally Elliott followed suit. So, I strapped everyone into their backpacks and off we went once more thorough the airport trying to make our way down to baggage claim. Jasmine was pushing the stroller while I held all of the kids. I must've looked like a dog-walker from Central Park because the looks I was getting from people were a bit odd. At this point in my day, I would've been open to any of their suggestions, but since none were being offered, we kept moving. Baggage claim was fun. *NOT!* Jeff had been at the airport in Houston to help us unload our entire mountain of stuff. It wasn't until the moment that I started grabbing suitcase after suitcase after car seat after suitcase after another car seat that I began to wonder, *How in the world am I going to get all of this stuff down to the rental car place? And please don't tell me there has to be a shuttle!* Seven suitcases, three car seats, one stroller, all of our carry-on stuff, three babies, one sitter, and a partridge in a pear tree later...I was exhausted, and when I turned to look at the kids, they actually *looked* like dogs by that point—dogs chasing their own tails. The newness of the backpacks had worn off, and they were trying to figure out how to take them off. They soon became most certain that the key to removing them was on their backs. So, they were all three walking in twisted circles with their little necks craned to the sides and arms up and over their heads trying (without success) to reach the head of the puppies. I had to laugh, *until I looked at the line for the rental car shuttle.*

I wanted to sit on the floor and cry, but I really didn't have time for that, so we loaded everything onto a trolley and headed for the door. I gave each kid something they could hold because it made them feel as though they were helping, and away we went. I think the time it took us to get our bags, go to the rental car place, and actually get our car, took almost as long as the entire flight from Houston to Orlando. And whose idea was it to come out here? Oh yeah. It was mine. Where is my husband? Missing all the fun. The rental car place messed up our reservation (go figure), but they made up for it and put us in a magical vehicle called a Grand Caravan. Apparently there's a difference between just a Caravan and a *Grand* Caravan. I don't drive a mini-van at home. I drive a monster

SUV. I mean, I practically need a step stool to get into the thing, but I'm telling you, this Grand Caravan was, well, *grand*. It had all sorts of hidden compartments. We fit all seven pieces of luggage into the back with room to spare and loaded the kids. I was certain we would have to strap one of them to the roof. Relax, we didn't have to…we all fit inside. We started making our way toward the resort. Did I mention that we were headed to Orlando at Spring Break? Do you know that it wasn't just Texas kids that were out of school for that week? Nope. It was kids from all over the place. The resort was a madhouse! It was another hour before we got settled into our condo. But again, it was worth the wait. During the unloading was where having a sitter was extremely handy. She kept the kids occupied while I tried to get everything in order. Right about the time I was putting the finishing touches on shoving the last suitcase in a closet, who walks through the door? Jeff. The kids went nuts: "Daddy!" "We rode on a airplane!" "I ate peanuts!" "I watched a movie!" "Ethan ran away from Mommy two times!" Jeff just looked at me and smiled. I collapsed on the couch.

• • • • • •

Our time at Disney World was interesting, to say the least. It's a lot like parenting. There are all sorts of things you can do while you are at Disney World that will make you laugh, cry, and want to throw up all at the same time. Just like parenting. One of the most obvious metaphors between Disney World and parenting is the roller coaster. I personally don't handle roller coasters very well. I'm nothing more than a big sissy-girl. My kids, on the other hand, are not afraid of anything. Unfortunately for them, they have peanuts for parents, so finding a roller coaster that they cleared the height requirement on was a trick. We managed to get Ethan and Emma on Goofy's Barn Burner roller coaster. Elliott was simply too much of a shrimp, which suited me fine. I stayed on the ground with him to watch.

How many times while we parent do we actually feel as though we are on a roller coaster? I know that I have felt that way many times, and it has not been something so mild as Goofy's Barn Burner. I could feel my feet leave the ground as I got tossed from one side to the next. I could feel my neck get whipped around from one thing to another. Maybe someone should have checked to see if I met the height requirement before I got pregnant with my first one!

We do a lot of waiting while we parent. We wait on two pink lines—we wait for them to sleep—we wait for them to talk—we wait for them to grow—most of the time we simply *wait*. Having visited Disney World during their absolute busiest/worst time of year, we did a lot of waiting in line. Everywhere we went, we waited in line: forty-five minutes here, thirty minutes there…but nowhere was the line longer or more slow-moving than when we went to see the Disney Princesses. They put the princesses in this ginormous tent. I think they do that so they have adequate room to wind all of us crazies halfway around the park so we won't clog too many of the main arteries to too many rides. We waited for an hour and a half. No joke. We stood in line and counted the birds on the walls. We held kids and talked to the other people in line. We sat on the floor and held kids. We took turns rotating out of line to go to the bathroom. We got snacks. Then, we had to go to the bathroom again. We sang songs, although not very well. For an hour and a half, we did this. The kids held up relatively well.

We finally made it to the cusp of the tent. The workers gave us our initial run down of how we were to proceed through the tent. We were to be orderly and calm...don't dawdle, be polite, smile for your picture, and keep the line moving. Sounds easy enough.

It's harder than you think.

There were three princesses in the tent. The first was Sleeping Beauty. She was charming and beautiful, just as you'd expect her to be. She thought Elliott was the cat's meow. She bent down and planted a great big kiss on his forehead. He squealed with delight. She was enamored by him. He was this round, blonde, blue-eyed, little angel who had fallen down from heaven. Who wouldn't want to just squeeze him? We had our photo-op with Sleeping Beauty with no issues. Next we moved on to Snow White. She, too, was just as beautiful as you'd expect her to be. Ethan and Emma were somewhat shy about approaching her with their autograph books in hand, but they obediently walked forward, handed her their books and posed for their pictures. Elliott hung back. He just stood there looking at her. She bent down to his level and with the skills that only a true princess could possess; she beckoned him closer with the promise of a secret. His big blue eyes got wider, and he moved closer to her; she gently cupped his chin, as though she were about to whisper the secrets of the king-dom in his ear... Then—without warning—she turned his little head and planted a huge smacker on his cheek!

He screamed so loud, everyone in the tent looked at us. He took her face in his pudgy little hands and said, "You trick me! Can I still know your secret?" She laughed and whispered something in his ear. To this day, I still don't know what she told him. We moved on to the final princess in the room.

Snow White promises Elliott the secrets to her kingdom, but surprises him with a kiss instead!

Proof that Elliott's time in line had not been wasted!

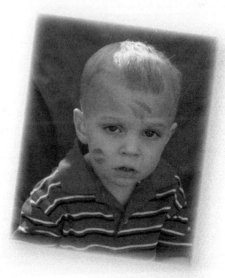

Ethan and Emma moved through the tent in a trance-like state of being in the presence of such fantastic royalty. Elliott was skipping from cloud to cloud, having been effectively tagged by two of the world's most famous princesses. Both his cheek and forehead had the lipstick stains to prove that his time waiting in line had not been wasted.

Each princess had been curtained off, so your view of the next princess was extremely limited. We knew we were coming into the final princess room; we just didn't know which princess we would be seeing. I mean, Disney World has a lot of princesses. We could've been waiting for Ariel or Jasmine...even Tinker Bell is considered to be a Disney Princess now. Emma was the first to get a peek. "Mommy! It's Cinderella! I see her! Mommy! It's Cinderella!" And that's when Elliott lost his mind.

Up to this point, Elliott had been content to wait his turn. He had allowed his sister to go first (we are trying desperately to teach the boys that "girls go first"), and then his brother. However, when he saw Cinderella standing there waiting for him, he lost all abandon! Cinderella was, and still is to this day—although he will not admit it—his favorite princess. He threw his arms wide to both sides, sending his brother and sister diving for cover, and took off in a run to greet his walking, talking, living dream. Cinderella turned to look at this pint-sized bundle of love coming at her, still bearing the marks of her sister princesses, and she bent down to receive the hug that was coming her way. A seemingly harmless gesture, right? Wrong. What poor Cindy failed to notice, was that in this slow-motion-run-to-hug that Elliott was doing, he had totally and completely dropped his left shoulder in a most impressive imitation of an NFL linebacker. So what appeared to be a sweet and innocent two-year-old, was, in fact, a compact stick of dynamite love getting ready to explode all over her! There was nothing I could do to stop it. Elliott slammed into her open arms, knocking her off her feet! She went over backwards, the hoops of her dress lifting Elliott even further up onto her chest. Princess secret service sprang into action, "Princess down! We have a princess down!" Emma screamed, "You broke her, Elliott!" Elliott had managed to wiggle himself up around her neck and now had her in a two-year-old head-lock. Jeff and I stood rooted to the spot. We couldn't even video this debacle. Princess secret service was trying (with no avail) to get Elliott to release his grip from around Cinderella's neck. They decided it was a lost cause, and picked the both of them up in one fluid motion.

**Elliott had Cinderella in a full-on headlock!
He refused to let his dream girl get away!**

Elliott still had not let go of his dream girl. Cinderella bent down and set him gently on the ground and pried him away from her neck. He just stood there staring into her eyes with unhidden love. Her secret service detail stood close by watching us with intense dislike. Cinderella looked at Elliott, and without missing a beat she said, "My! What a strong little prince you are!" And with that, she kissed the only remaining place left on his face...his other cheek. She posed for all the pictures with the kids, and then the secret service escorted us out.

How many times have we felt like that with our parenting? We wait and wait and wait for something...then, when we finally arrive at whatever it is we've been waiting for, we simply cannot contain ourselves! I've been there. For me, it was two pink lines. Then two more pink lines... Then (gasp!) two *more* pink lines! I wanted those babies. Then, when they got here, I wanted to just *watch* them. Granted, sometimes that was like waiting in line: A whole lotta standing around with not a lot going on. Then, other times, it was exactly like meeting Cinderella: I just couldn't contain myself. Still other times, it was like the Mad Hatter's Tea Party ride: better known as the spinning teacups.

We went on the Mad Hatter's Ride while we were at Disney World. The kids thought it would be a super-double-terrific-fun thing to do. I mean, have you seen all the pretty colored teacups? My husband was cracking up at the mere thought of me climbing into one of these cups. I don't *do* motion all that well. My stomach began to get very uneasy. For those of you who may not have had the pleasure of sitting in one of these Walt Disney multi-colored torture machines, please allow me to explain how they work. You approach a giant, flat-surfaced area that holds many, many multi-colored jumbo-sized teacups that have large steering wheels protruding up from the middle of the cup. It's all very pretty and pleasing to the eye, but then so was the field of poppies in *The Wizard of Oz*, and we all know where that landed Dorothy. Looks do not always reveal the true intent or purpose of an object. So, we all climbed aboard one of these seemingly harmless teacups (we could all fit into one) and got ready to ride around the track. It was a nice day. Kids were laughing. We could have been a commercial for Disney World up to this point. Then, without warning, the teacup began to spin rapidly on its track to the right, and my husband took the steering wheel and turned our cup to the left. We all whipped around and the kids went nuts. I could taste my lunch. The kids were screaming, "AGAIN! AGAIN! MORE! MORE!" I was praying this was one of the shorter rides at the Magic Kingdom. Back and forth we went. When the cup changed on its track to the left, we (and I do mean Jeff) spun the cup to the right. This went on for an eternity. I understand why there wasn't really a line at this ride. Spinning teacups: Around and around you go, where you'll stop, no one knows.

Now, I told you that story so I could tell you another one. The tale I'm about to tell you is true. I've not even changed the names to protect the innocent because as this series of events unfolds, you won't find any "innocents."

This story actually begins around midnight one Saturday evening. My husband and I had just returned home from a rodeo fundraising gala. Hey, we live in Texas: horses, cows... it's what we do. The Houston Livestock Show and Rodeo is one of the biggest and best rodeos in the world, and the pregame festivities are too good to miss! Upon arriving home, we were greeted at our house by a very sleepy Nana (a.k.a.: my mother-in-law, Carol). As we said our thank yous and goodbyes, she began looking for her shoes. Remembering that she had left them outside on the table while the kids were swimming, she went out into the backyard to get them, only to find they were no longer on the table. Grace, the latest addition to the family, a spunky three-and-a-half-month-old Golden Retriever puppy had decided that Nana's shoes looked too inviting to leave on the table. She was going through this hide-and-seek phase. Our other dog, Littles, was much older and more "seasoned," and completely nonplussed over the arrival of Nana's shoes. Typically, Grace didn't *eat* what she took, she just hid it. This was *not* amusing to us at midnight. I made the comment to my mother-in-law that I hoped they weren't her favorite shoes, to which she promptly replied that they were. *Terrific.* Jeff told her we would get her another pair, only to be told that they no longer make this particular type. *Double-terrific.* After thirty minutes of searching through flowerbeds, in the dark, dressed in black-tie attire, for *brown shoes*, we decided to look when we had a little bit more light. Nana put on her one shoe, limped with one shoe on to her vehicle, went home, and we went to bed. Can you feel the teacup beginning to spin?

The next morning, we did not make it to church (I'm thinking that is where my day went wrong); instead we stayed home and helped my husband pack for his business trip. Kids are such intuitive little machines and they know when Mommy or Daddy is running low on energy or patience and they don't hesitate to use that to their advantage. Once Jeff was gone, I tried to be the fun mommy that doesn't always come out. (I spend most of my days doing the less-glamorous side of motherhood, the side you don't see on daytime shows: the cooking, cleaning, laundry, carpool...the list goes on.) But, as we said our goodbyes to Daddy, I saw three very sad faces of kiddos that would rather have Daddy stay and play than have to wave goodbye to him for a three-day trip. Never fear! I had a plan! But as luck would have it, the visions of fun and sun that I had in my head were not to be.

Once we were all properly sun-screened, hatted, and hydrated, we headed into the backyard for a swim. Well, as I mentioned, we have a new puppy. Grace is a retriever—a *water* dog— and she thinks that anytime anyone gets near the pool, she, too, is invited in for a swim. The only problem with this train of thought is that she thinks the kids are floatation devices or fetch toys. This is not something that the kids are incredibly keen on. As I struggled with keeping Grace off of the younger two, Ethan, who was four years old at the time and had been swimming like a fish since he was two, chose *this* day to learn that when he went underwater, he could no longer hear my instructions.

The first time or two that he did this was, in all honesty, quite humorous. After all, he was learning a new way to eventually annoy his mother! But after repeating my instructions to him four or five times, it rapidly became less and less funny, and more and more irritating. Especially as I was struggling with two screaming babies and a dog that has mistaken their cries and flailing arms as personal invitations to play with even more bounce and spunk! Eventually, I got everyone out of the pool, and we made our way into the house for lunch and rest time.

Evidently, I'm not as bright as I look because after rest time we ventured back outside for more pool time. This time we were joined by our neighbors. Mike and Terri are wonderful people who love our children, and who do not have any children themselves. So, when they come to our house, it is, on days like this, a reassuring thought that they made the right choice in not opting for parenthood. Please don't get me wrong, I love my children dearly, but there are times when they test me almost beyond what I can bear. Grace was absolutely LOVING the fact that we not only had company, but that the company was playing with her and the fact that there were kids running everywhere was just an added bonus.

Apparently, Emma and Elliott were not really on board with the whole swim-without-crying-constantly-idea, so I made an executive decision to go inside. My teacup is gaining momentum. Can you feel it now? As I was telling...check that...as I was trying to tell Ethan the new game plan, he insisted on going underwater every time I opened my mouth. Mike and Terri found this incredibly entertaining; I, on the other hand, wasn't nearly so amused. After getting the babies out of the pool and sufficiently dried off, I stationed them by the back door and went back to the water's edge for Ethan who was still doing a very good impression of a bobbing apple. He was quite pleased with himself until I got back in the pool, picked him up out of the water, and carried him to where the towels were.

What came after this can only be described as a meltdown of epic proportions that could have easily been followed by, "I would like to thank the Academy..." Meanwhile, the babies have opened the back door and stepped slowly into the house in utter speechlessness and amazement at the massive fit their older brother is throwing. Emma seemed a bit in awe that it was, in fact, Ethan, and not herself putting on the elaborate show. She is usually my drama queen. Elliott was simply at a loss for sound or movement...he merely stood in silence to watch and see how this was going to end. Please bear in mind that although we were *technically* in the house, we were not so far in that I could close the back door, which gave Grace yet another invitation to become part of the action and not merely a spectator. In she came, bounding into me and a wilting Ethan, sliding across my kitchen tile, wet and muddy tail wagging, and jumping on Emma, who incidentally let out her own award-winning shriek. This brought Mike out of the pool to corral Grace back outside while trying (unsuccessfully) to hide a large grin and unconvincing cough cover-up.

Spinning teacups.

Have you ever tried to pick up a wet, screaming four-year-old who didn't want to be picked up? I think that I probably would've had more luck with a thirty-five-pound blob of Jell-O. "Slippery when wet" came to my mind. That "limp noodle" thing that kids do is highly effective in not allowing the parent a good grip. Ethan had melted into a screaming puddle on my floor. I had to resort to throwing a beach towel over him and scooping him up like I would a wild animal I was trying to get out of the house. This, let me assure you, wasn't something he expected; nor was it something he welcomed. It is an absolute miracle that the both of us made it up the stairs in one piece! By the time I finally managed to get him in his room and to actually stay in there, the other two had awoken from their shock and scrambled up the stairs to see what more would take place in this recent battle of wills between Mommy and Ethan.

Keep in mind that I was still dripping wet, heart racing, and very disappointed that the visions I had for a fun day with Mom was rapidly going from bad to worse. So, I did what any level-headed mother in a very frustrating situation would do: I put in a movie for the other two, and told them to stay upstairs. I closed the gate at the top of the stairs and took the baby monitor outside with me, so that I could go and apologize to my neighbors for the elaborate show that had just taken place.

As soon as I walked outside, here came Grace, just as happy as ever to see me, and Mike and Terri were losing all composure as I got closer to the pool. They weren't even trying to hold back the laughter that ensued! Which, seeing them having such a good chuckle, seemed to lighten my mood slightly and I joined in on the laughter. Terri looked at me and said, "You know I love your kids, but it is times like this that make me really glad that we can go home to an empty house!" I quickly asked if I could go with her. She laughed even harder.

Then, thanks to the wonders of technology, I heard the ever-present and all-too-familiar cry of "MOMMY!" I wanted so badly to answer back with, "She's not here!" I knew that my short-lived break was over, and I had to retreat back into the house...back into the duties that I couldn't hand off to anyone else because Daddy was gone for the next three days. My heart sank a little lower in my chest. Turns out, Emma and Elliott had, in fact, snapped out of their momentary loss of speechlessness and peaceful coexistence. My little piranha, who we affectionately refer to as Elliott, had taken a bite out of his sister over a toy of some sort. Emma had more teeth marks on her than Grace's favorite chew toy. You would think she'd learn not to let him get that close to her! Once that issue was resolved (a Care Bear band-aid on the finger seemed to cure the bite on her arm), Ethan opened his door and announced that he was ready to be good. And also, he would like to have spaghetti for dinner. Since I had no other plans for dinner, spaghetti worked for me, too.

In our house, and I would wager that in most houses where toddlers live, spaghetti is a finger food. But apparently, Emma had been paying a little too much attention to the way that Grace eats *her* food, because this was the night that she began sucking her spaghetti off of her plate with her mouth. Elliott promptly followed suit. By this time of the day, I had neither the energy nor the inclination to stop this madness. They were eating—they were not fighting—and that was all that mattered to me at that point. However, once dinner was over, the chaos resumed.

Will this ride ever stop?

The kids had gotten into this bad habit of chasing each other through the downstairs while I clean the kitchen. It had become a nightly ritual. This was not a safe choice and it was not something that Jeff or I condoned, but on this particular night, I lacked the strength to stop it. As the kids were running (and I do mean *running*), there was a collision—several to be exact. They ran into each other, they ran into the walls, and they even bumped into the island in the middle of the kitchen floor. I heard cries of annoyance and mild irritation, but nothing major. Naturally, about this time the phone rings; of course it was Daddy calling to check in. *Where do I even begin?* So many things had happened that day that I was beyond words to even begin to describe all of things that the kiddos had done. After I had been on the phone with him for all of fifteen seconds, I heard Ethan's voice from the other room, "I'm sorry I'm sorry I'm sorry," followed by *that* scream. You know the scream I'm talking about: the *blood-curdling* scream that comes from the place so deep within your child that he cannot move and it is usually accompanied with breath-holding. I totally hung up on my husband and found Elliott face-down on the tile, Ethan standing beside him, and Emma just rounding the corner to check out the action. No longer at a loss for words, I lash out at my oldest while instinctively picking up the baby from the floor (fully expecting to see blood, which, thankfully, there wasn't any). "WHAT DID YOU DO TO HIM?!" Not one of my bright and shining moments of motherhood. "Nothin'," was the first answer I got. But, as I dragged him once again up the stairs, he told me he *may* have pushed his little brother down. Judging from the massive knot that was forming over Elliott's left eye, I would say "body slam" would be a more accurate word. After Ethan was securely placed in his room again, I turned my attention on the now purple lump swelling on Elliott's head. He had stopped crying, and was now whimpering.

Ice. He needed ice on his head. So, I put some frozen peas in a Ziploc sandwich bag and rubber-banded them in a cloth diaper. Remarkably, he kept them on his head for awhile. I took both him and Emma upstairs to Emma's room and propped him up on pillows to watch *Aladdin* so that I could go explain to Ethan why body-slamming his little brother is not a good idea. After that, I went back downstairs to try and finish cleaning up the kitchen.

I was almost done. I could see the light at the end of the tunnel that was my day, when I heard Ethan from the top of the stairs, "Mom, the babies made a mess in Elliott's room with the peas!" I told him that I would be there in a minute. Wiped counter. Got cups out of drawer to make their night-time milk. "Mom! Elliott poo-poo in my bed!" This came from Emma.

I absolutely froze.

And thought, *Please God, what are you trying to do to me today?*

Spinning teacups.

I asked Ethan if Elliott still had on a diaper. He assured me that he did, but there was still poo-poo in Emma's bed and I needed to come upstairs right away. I grabbed a plastic grocery bag from the pantry and headed upstairs to see what was waiting for me in Emma's room. Thankfully, when I walked into Emma's room, I found that the big upset was a chocolate milk stain, and Elliott wasn't even dirty. As I turned to leave the room, I noticed five or six peas on the floor and remembered that Ethan told me there was more in Elliott's room. I figured since I was already upstairs I might as well go and pick them up; after all I *did* have the grocery bag with me.

When I reached the door of Elliott's room, I stopped dead in my tracks. "Mess" did not even come *close* to what was waiting for me on the floor of that room. It looked as though a bomb of once-frozen peas had exploded all over the place. I didn't think that I had put that many peas in that little baggie. Apparently I did. I dropped to my knees and began the tedious task of picking up peas one-at-a-time. Enter Emma and Elliott followed by Ethan saying, "See, I told you there was a mess in here." Well, Emma and Elliott wanted to "help." But unfortunately, what they did was anything but that! As they walked across the room, the peas that at one time were frozen have now thawed out, which made them much easier to squish as they were stepped on by chubby little feet. My patience was gone at this time. I yanked Elliott up and put him in the rocking chair in his room and sent Emma, rather forcefully, to her room. And I proceeded picking up the peas.

The phone rang.

Remember the missing shoe? It was Nana calling to ask me if I had looked for it, and if so, had I managed to find it?

Simple question. Justified question. Way wrong time for me to answer it with a level head. I snapped at her as I informed her that no, I had not found it, and yes, I had looked for it along with my neighbors and Ethan. The only thing that I did not do was dig up the sandbox which is the only logical place it could be, but considering we were talking about a puppy, the word *logical* didn't really seem to fit in any capacity. I told her that I had asked Ethan to dig up the sandbox to which he replied, "But, Momma, what am I supposed to do with the sand after I take it out of the sandbox?" I then assured her that I would dig it up tomorrow, and we would find the missing shoe.

Pause.

Breathe.

I apologized and told her what I was in the process of doing, and why, and that I would talk to her later. I hung up and resumed my pea-picking adventure. Fifteen minutes later, I was pretty sure that I had managed to find all of the peas that were scattered all over the floor, and had now tucked them safely away in the plastic grocery bag. Here's where it gets fun... I want you to have a good, clear mental picture of this: I was holding the top of the bag in one hand, and I took hold of the bottom of the bag and give it a good spin so I can tie the top of it in a knot. Well, unbeknownst to me, the bag had a hole in it that is just big enough for... you guessed it: peas to fit through. I have now re-scattered about twenty peas back over the floor that I just picked up!

And my teacup spins faster...

Elliott rushes to my rescue and in the process of "helping" me, he smashed the soft peas into my beige carpet leaving tiny green spots everywhere. This reduced me to tears. Peas!

Again, I get all of them picked up, but this time I was hold-ing the escaped peas in my hand while I headed downstairs to finish the other tasks that I started hours ago and never managed to finish. Finally, after many attempts, the kids were finally in bed. I was exhausted.

As I was getting the house and dogs ready for bed, I opened the back door to let the dogs inside, and something just off the edge of the patio catches my eye: Nana's missing shoe! You would've thought that I had discovered the cure for cancer! I was so excited that something had gone right. I raced over and picked it up to examine it; it was in perfect condition. Not a tooth mark on it. Apparently, Grace had merely hidden it for safe-keeping. It was the hide-and-seek phase.

The next few days were fairly uneventful. Daddy returned home, and the kids put their angel-faces on again. And Nana got her shoe back. The moral of this story is: No matter how hard you try to make your own plans, kiddos have their own agenda, and that usually doesn't coincide with yours. Oh, and don't wear your favorite and irreplaceable shoes to a house with three kids, a swimming pool, and a new puppy.

That was one day I was hoping would not repeat itself. Naturally, we had other days to compete for the Worst Day Ever title. But, as I'm going for the metaphor of Disney World right now, that one will have to do.

Children will do the darnedest things. They will make you think you're going crazy. They will also help you understand why some animals eat their young. Take fish for example. Fish have babies. *Lots* of babies. If you've ever owned a fish tank with a boy guppy and a girl guppy, then you know that fish have babies. Why, then, do they *eat* those babies? Beats me. Population control, perhaps. Or maybe it's the whole bumper car scenario within the tank. Fish tend to give a whole new meaning to the term "multiple births," therefore, over-crowding becomes a bit of an issue...kind of like the bumper cars.

We also rode the bumper cars while at Disney World. Mainly because the kids also cleared the height requirement on this ride, too. They had a ball slamming into each other. I was a nervous wreck just watching them. And all the while I was driving my car that was being pummeled by other drivers, I was thinking about other cases where there are just too many people around to be able to concentrate on just *one*. The point of this book is to give you encouragement so you can survive parenting while your kids are little. So many of the things I'm sharing with you happened when my kids were very young. Don't get me wrong, they haven't moved out and gotten jobs or anything at the time of this writing, but they have (thankfully) outgrown some of the antics found nestled within these pages.

When you're on a bumper car track, it is impossible to watch everyone else on the track who might be coming your way. When you have three or more children out in public anywhere, you face the same challenges. When two people have two children, they are still operating on man-to-man defense. Meaning: one kid per adult. When you throw a third kid into that mix, suddenly, as parents, you are outnumbered, and you begin operating on a zone defense. Meaning: one parent will have two kids.

This is where we found ourselves while at a birthday party when we were potty-training Elliott. Jeff was in the pool with Ethan because, let's face it, Ethan was the easy one. I was supposed to be watching the babies. I *was* watching them...to an extent. I knew approximately where they were. They both had proper pool floatie suits on, plus there were scores of other parents, so if one of them wandered to the pool side, I would know or someone would grab them. Well, Elliott was a bit more elusive than I gave him credit for. I was caught up in a conversation with another parent, and before I knew it, the hostess mom tugged on my arm to alert me to the exact location of my son. He was standing in the middle of her patio, shorts around his ankles, peeing on the stick of the umbrella that was stuck through one of her tables. I thought parents were supposed to be able to embarrass their kids...not the other way around. It's been years since that happened, and it still gets brought up at pool parties we go to. They make absolutely sure we know where the bathrooms are. Some people are so funny...

. . . . . .

As it turns out, Elliott and Ethan are not the only ones who have the capability to blindside me with their antics. Emma turned in a whopper of her own. She just chose a much more elegant setting. Picture this: one black-tie wedding, three precious children (mine—two in miniature tuxedos and one in a dress perfectly crafted to match the bride), and one dignified and tastefully decorated reception hall. What could possibly go wrong? Have you ever heard the phrase, "Looks like country has come to town"? It means that someone let the less refined section of society mingle with those more accustomed to shiny and sparkly karats rather than orange and dirty carrots fresh from the ground. At any rate, we fell into the category of: "Who invited *them*?" This doesn't really bother me. I typically don't have too much trouble adjusting to a higher society. I prefer real people, but when I have to, I can sit at a formal dinner and look presentable. I know which fork to use, *Pretty Woman* was most helpful, and I know how to make intelligent small talk. My children, on the other hand, were a bit too young to realize that there are some things many in this particular setting would frown (greatly) upon.

My brother-in-law was getting married. He and his bride-to-be sweetly asked Jeff and I if the kids could be in the wedding party. Naturally, we said yes. I was thrilled to be going to such a fancy affair. I love getting dressed up and looking like a girl, instead of the tired mommy I parade around as most days. The kids looked great for their big event, too. Emma was the perfect picture of a little princess. The boys did their part very well during the ceremony. No one really fidgeted too much. Emma was one of two flower girls, and I'm excited to say that the "accident puddle" that appeared on the floor in the general vicinity of my daughter was not her doing. It was the other one. Things were going great. The wedding went well; no one passed out. I took a deep breath.

Then we moved from the chapel to the reception hall. This place was beautiful. It had floor-to-ceiling windows that overlooked a magnificent garden that was backed by some of the tallest trees that East Texas has to offer. The whole place could've been a movie set. Inside the room, off to one side, was a huge, curved staircase that led from the second floor where the bride and groom would make their grand entrance all the way down to the reception. This wasn't a sit-down dinner, but rather many different stations along each wall. Some had fruit, others had veggies, still others had sweets. Next to the fruit station was a chocolate fountain, which is where my children spent most of their time. I began to wander through the room, I was really looking for the chocolate fountain, when I came upon a small crowd of people near the foot of the stairs. Being the nosey woman that I am, I moved closer to investigate. I was met by the wedding coordinator, my new sister-in-law, her mother (who looked liked she'd eaten something bitter every time she saw me), the wedding photographer, some other random people, and a couple of well-dressed little boys. The spectacle that everyone was gawking at?: A lovely miniature vision in a white flower girl's dress doing her best swan dive from the fifth stair up on that beautiful curved staircase. She hit the floor with a resounding smack! The photographer turned to the crowd in general and announced, "I got it that time!" The wedding coordinator, my brand new sister-in-law, and her ill-tempered mother all turned to look at me as I stared down at my laughing daughter, lying spread-eagle on the floor. I opened my mouth, but nothing came out. I swallowed, squared my shoulders, and said, "Someone should go find her father." I spun on my heels, hiked up my dress, stepped over my laughing child, and went in search of the champagne fountain, figuring it would taste better than chocolate.

Times like these are exactly why some animals eat their young.

Summer, 2004

Most families in our neighborhood cruise the streets in golf carts...not us! We tool the 'hood on a four-wheeler! It drives the neighbors crazy.

Alien Adventures
& Other UFOs

(Unique Family Occasions)

Have you ever looked at your child and thought, *Where in the world did he come from?* Or, *There's no way she can possibly be* **mine**.... Or thoughts such as: *They don't do anything the way that* I *do; They don't act the way that* I *do; I never did any of the wretched things that* **they** *do; Of these things, I am absolutely sure.*

Two words: Oh, really?

You see, when we get married and decide to have these wonderful little miracles running around our house, we forget that it isn't only our DNA that courses through their little bodies. Granted, you may have been the poster child for perfect children everywhere that fairytales were indeed written for and about...but what about your Uncle Irvine on your mother's side, twice removed, that shows up at the family reunion, and who insists upon wearing the muumuu he bought *that one time* he visited Hawaii in 1968 because it feels breezy when the wind blows? Did you forget about him? His DNA is hard wired into Junior's makeup as well as yours...and that, sweet sister, will make for one interesting child concoction. Betcha forgot to mention your dear, sweet, old Uncle Irvine to your hubby before y'all thought about procreation. It's precisely those obscure (and some not so obscure, i.e., your mother) relatives that I want to bring to your attention over the next few pages.

Alien adventures. Sometimes it will most certainly feel like we've entered a parallel universe. I watch, well I don't actually *watch*, but I do have the privilege to *listen to* a lot of Star Wars at my house. I confess, I've never really gotten all that into it. I can't keep track of who belongs on which side, but my oldest son...now *he* can tell you exactly who the Republic fights for and who fights for the Empire (which, by the way, I had to run downstairs and ask about those sides while I was typing this out). There are times when I simply have to stand back and shake my head at the whole lot of them! The upside to the whole Star Wars thing is the interest in space that has been sparked in my house. Space...the final frontier. I know I'm crossing my science fiction a bit, but bear with me for a minute. I do know that particular line came from Star Trek and not Star Wars. The bottom line is that space is really, *really* big. Our families can be really, *really* big as well. In the beginning, the boys were a little concerned that remnants of the Death Star would be falling into our swimming pool at any given moment, until I assured them that it was blown up somewhere over New York state and we were perfectly safe down here in Texas. Then they were fine. Apparently

they weren't all that worried about the people of New York...
perhaps I should've been more troubled by their lack of concern than I was at the time...I apologize to our friends from
the north. But, it was through their curiosity of the Death
Star that they became very interested in other things that
might be in our Solar System...things a bit more real.

I wanted to share some of those things with you because
it occurred to me that while this was an awesome teachable
moment for my boys, thinking back on this moment became
an excellent teachable moment for us, as parents. Let me
explain. Now, don't panic. This is going to be fun. I'm not
going to turn this into a long and drawn out analogy of a science class that many of us slept through in high school the
first time around, so why would this be any different? I promise to make this fun and we just might learn a little something
along the way.

Did you know that things are still being discovered in our
solar system? Well, when I say "discovered," I'm not talking
yesterday, but I do mean recently, some even in my lifetime,
and contrary to what my children think...it wasn't all *that*
long ago. For instance, Pluto wasn't discovered until 1930.
That was less than one hundred years ago! When you com-
pare one hundred years to the age of the universe, that's like
the blink of an eye. Did you know that Jupiter has rings?
Those were discovered in 1979, which *does* happen to be in
my lifetime. Then, in 2006, an astute group of brainiacs got
together and discussed and decided on the "official" qualifications of a planet, thus disqualifying poor Pluto as a real
planet. He was downgraded to a "dwarf" planet. Can I get a
collective, "oooohhhhhh"? If they were looking for something

to occupy their time with, they should've called me. I've got loads of stuff for them...literally...loads. They could've done my laundry, rather than sit around trying to figure out the exact qualifications of a planet.

Stay with me as we move from the textbook science realm of discovery to the more abstract realms of discovery. What do my findings have to do with parenting? Plenty. I'll show you. Let's start with discovery. How many new talents and abilities have you discovered since you became a parent? I mentioned in a previous chapter that I learned how to do many things one-handed. The household chores do not stop because you've got a hungry baby. Dishes still needed to be loaded into the dishwasher. Even as high-tech as that machine is, it will not open the door by itself, jump up, and load those dishes from the sink onto its racks. My husband calls my way of loading the dishwasher "Dish Tetris"; he even gives me points for how many dishes I can shove in there without stacking. I discovered after having my children that I can hear sounds normal human beings cannot, and when I say "normal," I mean male. I can hear a baby crying from the neighbor's house through two closed front doors with televisions on in both houses. The amazing thing about this feat is that my husband (bless his heart) was in the same house as the crying child and could not hear said baby wailing. "I thought he was playing," says Hubby. Yep. Playing. He does that. The purple and red blotches on his face are happy colors that emerge as he tries to get your attention. Just like Jupiter, I discovered that I have new rings, too...although, I wasn't nearly as excited about my new rings as scientists were about Jupiter's. My rings began to appear in 2001...under my eyes. At first, I thought my makeup remover was cheap and not doing its job at removing my mascara. Then as the days and weeks wore on, I began to slowly comprehend the situation. It was much, much, *much* worse than un-removed makeup. My new rings were permanently placed under my eyes. They were dark, they were purple, and evidently they were not going anywhere. Concealer now had to be applied before *and* after my foundation in order to cover the atrocities that the sleep deprivation was doing to me. That was in 2001. It's now more than ten years later and those rings are still with me even though the newborns are not so "new" anymore.

But really, when you think about it, sleep is highly overrated. Although, I *would* like to take this opportunity to reverse every mean thing I ever said to my mother and preschool teacher each and every time they tried to get me to take a nap when I was a kid. Unfortunately, you cannot stockpile sleep minutes and then make withdrawals as you need them. It'd be totally cool if you could, though. I would make one of those withdrawals today. Today is the second consecutive day that I am operating on an interrupted night of sleep.

The night before last, my oldest son decided to read a book just before bed that involved a giant, six-foot-tall, man-eating rat. That should make for a peaceful night's sleep, don't you think? Not! Somewhere around three thirty in the morning, I got a tug on my arm. "Mom...are you awake?" I jolted out of a dead-sleep and jumped two feet in the air. Of course I was awake. Why wouldn't I be awake at—check the clock—three thirty in the morning?! "I had a bad dream." You think? A giant, six-foot-tall, man-eating rat that happens to guard some distant castle where a princess is being held captive was giving him nightmares? I never would've guessed it. So, into bed with my husband and me he came. Let us just pause right there. My husband and I have never shared a bed with our children. Only under extreme circumstances were they allowed to sleep in our *room*, and that was on a pallet on the floor. Having a child in our bed meant that the child was between me and my husband. This is not a healthy dynamic for any marriage, under any circumstance; we will talk more about that in a later chapter. However, at three thirty the other morning, Ethan climbed over me and into bed between the both of us, and no one got any sleep for the rest of the night. Last night, I made an executive Mom decision to ban all giant, man-eating rat books, and decree that nighttime books must be benign with bunnies and butterflies so as not to upset the delicate sleep patterns that belong to Mom. I thought I had done a fairly good job with my new marching orders until...the tug...and, "Mom...are you awake?" I rolled over and peeled the sandpaper off the inside of my eyelids, and looked into the face of a different child. Emma was look-ing back at me. "I had a bad dream." *Man-eating rats?* I won-dered quietly to myself. I looked at the clock; it was three fifteen in the morning. Awesome. I was beginning to think the kids were holding nightly meetings to see whose turn it would be to poke the sleeping monster. Evidently, Emma had drawn the short straw.

I'm also discovering that while they seem to believe that I do not require sleep, my husband (who also doubles as their father) has the ability to morph into an invisible and supremely evasive nocturnal being, with powers so stealthy as to evade capture by the aliens that had invaded our once peaceful and quiet habitat. In other words: they never wake up Daddy! Just me, it's always me! Can anyone tell me why that is?! Out of bed I came, taking Emma by the hand, and together we walked back up the stairs and into her room. Fool me once, shame on you; fool me twice, shame on me. I wasn't going to have a kiddo in bed with me two nights in a row. We made it to her room, turned on a nightlight, got the standard and most magical drink of water, and I tucked her back into bed. Just so you don't think I am positively the meanest mother in the world, I did sit with her for a while, stroking her hair until she was almost asleep before exiting her room. I checked on the boys and then made my way down the stairs to tumble back into bed to rest my eyes for another forty-five minutes before my alarm launched into song, reminding me it was time to greet the day. My husband merely groaned as he rolled over, still lost in peaceful and undisturbed slumber. How does he do it?

· · · · · ·

When my kids were babies, Jeff and I decided that it was best for me to stay home with them. I went from working full time, to staying home full time, with three itty-bitty, teeny-tiny little ones that seemed to cry constantly. Yes, this was what I had asked for, but no, this didn't appear to be what I had signed up for. Where was the fun? Where were the happy babies who played by themselves? Why were my kids always sick? Why didn't my husband bond instantly with our kids? They were *his* kids, too. I wanted—no, check that—I *craved* adult interaction. I talked to my kids all day long, but there simply isn't much conversation to be had with a two-year-old. I was feeling like Pluto. I had been downgraded.

I was a dwarf planet, stuck in the outermost realm of my solar system—alone, freezing, and wallowing in self-pity. I resembled something that looked like the other women, but my qualities were somehow less-than. Or so I thought... This is where the pharmaceutical intervention came into play. My thoughts and feelings of less-than were a combination of the hormonal chemical warfare raging inside my body combined with two years of sleep deprivation. I became delusional.

I knew the plan and the path that I was on was the right one. It was the path that God had ordained for me. It was the path and the plan that Jeff and I had discussed and decided would work best for our family. I mean, seriously, look at the cost of daycare for three infants! Infants often cost more than children from toddler age and up (not to mention the fact that most daycare facilities are only legally allowed a maximum of two infants at a time, so by the time you consider that most daycares have at least one already, it's likely that the kids would have ended up in three different daycares for a few years, and that's a gas bill all by itself). My entire paycheck would go straight to daycare! The majority of my feelings of downgraded-ness (is that even a word?) could be solved by a trip to my doctor and a nap. I look back on those early years when all the kids were so little (after I break out into a cold sweat) and think about the memories I missed. I was so tired. There were so many of them (kids). They were so little. I never slept. The whole house seemed to be in survival mode. It was a definite adventure.

We've seen how the physical aspect of parenting is like

an alien adventure—but now let's go beyond... Let's take a peek at some of our own *close encounters of the third kind*... some UFOs better known as extended family and *in-laws*. Each stage of parenting is an adventure. Each stage brings with it a new set of challenges, a new set of aliens, some *close encounters of the third kind*, and new UFOs to gawk at. When I thought (there were a couple of false alarms in there) that I was in labor with my daughter, Jeff and I spent one night walking the floors of the hospital. I really wanted Emma out; I was ready to *not* be pregnant anymore. Emma really likes to be in control. (Wonder where she gets that from?) She liked it that way while I was pregnant; she still likes it that way now. The apple doesn't fall far from the tree.

Anyway, as I was walking the halls, I wanted to talk to my mother. It was a perfectly natural request. I didn't have my cell phone with me, but that was alright; Jeff had his. I was flipping through his contact list looking for my mother's name. This is the problem with speed dial. When I was a kid, I knew everyone's name and number *by heart*. Now, I have them in my phone, and if I call you all the time, you're in my "favorites," so I don't even have to remember your last name. So, at the time of my floor-pacing episode with Emma, I couldn't find my mother's name. Don't panic...I do remember my mother's last name—even her first name on certain days.

I didn't expect my husband to have her listed in his phone under "Mother," but after several minutes of searching, several fairly strong contractions, and a fuse that was burning faster by the minute, I threw the phone at him and shouted, "I WANT TO TALK TO MY MOTHER! I KNOW YOU HAVE HER IN YOUR PHONE! WHERE IS SHE?!" He took the phone, righted it (as he'd barely had time to catch the thing before it hit the ground), and calmly scrolled through his contact list. He handed it to me in a matter of seconds and said, "Baby, she's right here. Under 'Outlaw.'" I just stared at him. Looking back, I can see the humor and the appropriateness of the nickname. It totally fits. At the time, on that night...it was not funny.

With that said, it's definitely time to visit the subject of outlaws and in-laws and *close encounters of the third kind* when we look at surviving parenting. It's wonderful to have access to as many generations as possible. When my kids were born, they were they the fifth generation on my side of the family alive. It was super cool. There's not really a handbook on what to do with that many people. How do you talk to that many people? What do you do when you all get together? What happens if one level or generation begins to lose their mind? That's where I'd like to pick up.

Even though my kids were the fifth generation, our family quickly slimmed down to only a couple of generations. We lost some matriarchs very soon after my youngest was born, one being my great-grandmother, then my grandmother, then my grandfather; those last two were the parents of my mother— the Outlaw. Well, having both of her parents gone on ahead to glory, Mother decided to make some changes. Changes that I never in a million years saw coming.

I come from a long line of self-employed folks. We are driven. We are hard workers. My parents are no exception. For the past twenty-five years, my parents have been a staple in north Austin (that's in Texas, y'all) with not one, but *two* highly successful restaurants. One of them was the Little Deli, which started as a moveable trailer in a parking lot. It was the bane of my existence every summer while I was in middle school, as I was sentenced to work there every day throughout the summers and then my sentence was extended to after school once I passed my driver's test and acquired a license. From the humble beginnings of that little trailer, hence the name *Little* Deli, they moved into a more permanent space in the shopping center to which they'd previously only held a spot in the parking lot. Business boomed.

Several years later, a new restaurant space opened up down the road from their house, and they converted that into a quaint little Italian neighborhood eatery. Thankfully by the time *It's Italian* opened, I had already moved to Houston, and could no longer be forced into schlepping drinks or carrying heavy food-laden trays. My three younger sisters, however, were not so lucky. The parents hired all three of them for various roles in both locations, and prided themselves on being family owned *and* operated. Both restaurants were critically acclaimed all across Austin. The Austin-American Statesman (newspaper) wrote articles about the food, the charm, and the ambiance of both places. Life was busy, but life was good. I promise all of this background information is important.

I received a phone call from my mother one afternoon. I'd like to replay that phone call for you now:

Phone rings

Me: Hello?

Mother: (She spoke in a very excited voice.) I have wonderful news!

Me: Okay. (I muffled the phone.) Ethan don't throw that...

Mother: We sold the Deli!

Me: (Choke!) You did what?!

Mother: We sold the Deli! Tony, from down the street, bought it!

Me: Mother, are you ill? Where's Dad? Does he know about this?

Mother: Yes! We sold the restaurant, too!

Me: (I walked into my room, closed the door, and sat on the floor.) *Why?*

Mother: We put the house on Craig's List...

Me: Mother, don't move. I'm coming.

Mother: Why? I'm fine. Your dad and I are going to truck-driving school.

Me: I'm sorry...you're going to do *what*?

Mother: Truck-driving school. We're going to become big rig truckers.

Me: Again, Mom, I have to ask: *Why?*

Mother: Well, we want to see the country. An RV is too expensive; this way we get paid. Oh, and we're sending your youngest sister to Houston to live with you.

I hung up.

Close encounters of the third kind.

Who does something like that? Who walks away from a twenty-five-year successful business to become an over-the-road trucker? My parents. They did go to truck-driving school. I didn't know there were schools for this sort of thing. Kind of makes me feel better to know that, though. I see those big rigs on the road: They've got all eighteen wheels turning, so it's nice to know they've been taught how to drive. I asked my mother if the company she and Dad landed at was going to block the gas pedal for her... Mother stands in at (barely) five-foot-tall. She didn't think that was very funny. I did. They bought a huge, fire-engine-red semi-truck.

Mother & Daddy in 2009, just before striking out to see America, trucker-style!

The house didn't sell on Craig's List...thankfully. They did have to enlist the help of an actual realtor. But that left a couple loose ends: three to be exact. I have three younger sisters. My sisters are much, *much* younger than I am. Mother was totally *not kidding* when she said she was sending the youngest to Houston. Jeff and I could have said no right there on the spot, but I honestly thought somewhere in my mind that having Kristina around would be/could be fun. It was right around the time that Mom and Dad decided to go crazy...I mean change careers... My twenty-year-old baby sister really did move in.

Let me just take this opportunity to say that there is most certainly a reason why God gives your children to you as babies, and NOT as twenty-year-olds. If they came to us as twenty-year-olds, our population would be on a significant and irrevocable rapid decline. I love my sister. Amazingly enough, I *still* love my sister, but there were times during her incarceration—I mean...her *stay*...here with us that I envisioned mailing pieces of her back to my parents. She was supposed to be with us for about nine or ten months; this would have been long enough to attend cosmetology school to get her license in hair design.

Eighteen months later, due to a *slight* lack of focus, she had not finished school, thus no license had been acquired. I did not have the help around the house that I had been promised to have *before* her arrival *and* on top of all of this—I had yet another body to clean up after and one more mouth to feed. My mom radar was going off nightly between two and three o'clock in the morning, alerting me to the fact that she still had not made it home, which kicked into high gear the worry factor and the hallucination stage of the *Oh-my-goodness-what-will-my-mother-do-to-me-if-something-happens-to-my-sister-on-my-watch?* phase. Something had to change. *Close encounters of the third kind*...the party-all-night-kind.

By this point, my parents and my other two sisters had decided to set up their home base in sunny California (which could get its own chapter for *close encounters*—I like California, but Texans and Californians are *very* different), so with the most diplomatic tone that I could muster, I called my mother and told her if she wanted her youngest daughter in one reusable piece and not a bag of confetti, she needed to point that big rig in the direction of Houston and come and get her.

Kristina, who also doubled as a human jungle-gym.

My nerves simply could not handle being the parent of a now-twenty-one-year-old. I had my hands full with my six-, seven-, and eight-year-olds, even though the behavior among the four of them was quite similar. Bottom line: I am now all by myself in Texas, as my entire immediate family is thirteen hundred miles away in California. Roll theme music—*All By Myself*...fade out...

Now if you thought it was just going to be the family on *my* side who was going to be compared to extraterrestrial life forms, guess again. Oh, no. My sweet mother-in-law has also provided me with ample material to add to this chapter. Carol lived with us for about a year and a half, and the help that she afforded me during that time provides her with a fair amount of immunity when it comes to the ribbing and the poking part of this book. With that said, there is one area of her life that is simply too good to pass up.

Around the same time that my parents took a leap off the

midlife crisis cliff, it became abundantly clear that they called Carol and had her drink the same Kool-Aid. I swear it was within a couple of months of receiving my mother's phone call that Jeff came home looking as though he'd been hit by a bus. I thought something terribly devastating had happened. I asked him, with a lump in my throat and my stomach in a knot, what had happened...thinking maybe someone died. He said, "Mom bought a bike." Me, in all of my wisdom and naiveté thought, *Hmmm, that's nice. She can get some exercise. It'll be good for her*, which is what I told him. He just stared back at me with a completely blank expression. He said, "No, Babe. A *bike*. A motorcycle. Like a Harley. But she didn't get a Harley, and doesn't like them, so don't ever, *ever* confuse her Honda with a Harley." Again, I had to sit down. *Close encounters of the third kind.* What was going on with my family?

Carol took a motorcycle safety class the very first weekend she had her bike. For that, I was grateful. At least both sets of grandparents were into the safety thing! The kids thought the fact that Nana rode a motorcycle and Granny and Papaw drove a big rig was just too cool for words. Jeff and I wondered when, exactly, our roles had been reversed, and *we* became the responsible ones...when did *we* become the parents of our parents?

Come to find out, you can't simply just own a motorcycle. To really understand the bike, you have to become *one* with the bike, and in order to do that you must be able to take it completely apart and then (ideally) put it back together with few leftover parts. Soon, I began saving my gallon milk jugs, and not for the igloo projects that my children built once a year at school, but rather for the break-down parties that

Nana held at her house. They needed something to drain the oil into, and milk jugs seemed to work the best. Who knew? She got connected with a "chapter" (my guess is that it's a group of other folks who ride), and they go tooling around the Texas hill country. I'm glad she doesn't often go out alone. I'm a huge believer in the old saying, "There's safety in numbers." She knows how to handle her bike. She wears her protective gear, and we keep buying her new helmets for Christmas— not because she wears them out (thankfully) but because she wants the latest and greatest, and she pays attention. That's about as good as we can expect. I honestly *can* tell you that, without a doubt, I did not see this type of alien adventure coming my way: motorcycle people and truck drivers. Does it get any crazier than that?

Nana riding the Tail of the Dragon in Tennessee, 2011.

• • • • • •

Something else that is widely talked about in space is UFOs. I personally don't really believe that little green men are flying around in spaceships, but I also didn't think my parents or my mother-in-law would do the about-face that they did either. What do I know? The kind of UFOs that I'm talking about are a little bit different than flying saucers. I'm talking about Unique Family Occasions. Anytime you mix two different bodies of people together, interesting things are going to happen. Can I just tell you that I'm tickled pink that Jeff doesn't spook easily? The very first time I brought him home to meet my family was a nightmare by female standards. He took it in stride—I was mortified. I met Jeff while I was living in Houston. My entire family, as you know, lived in Austin. I knew within a couple of dates that I'd met my match; he was "the one," my Prince Charming—pick a cliché. I knew I was going to have to take him home to meet the parents sooner or later.

We'd been dating for about three weeks when I called my mother and told her I was coming home for the weekend, and I was bringing Jeff with me. She was shocked speechless. I had not brought anyone home in years. Literally, *years*. She wanted to know if I had drugged him. (To know my mother is to love her.) I begged her not to scare him off, to please have Daddy be on his best behavior, and told her we'd see them on Saturday. As we were on the road making the two-and-a-half-hour trip from Houston to Austin, my cell phone rings. It was my mother. She just wanted to let me know that she was really excited to see us, and to give me a little warning that there may be *a few* people at the house when we arrive.

My heart sank. I know my parents. At this point in their lives, they were heavily engrossed in the restaurant/catering business. Any time Mother mentioned "a few," that could easily be translated into at least fifty. I wanted to turn around, but as we were more than halfway to Austin, we kept going.

When we got to my parents' subdivision, I was desperately trying to remain calm. I had a couple of different factors working against me, the first being that they had not lived in this house for very long, and my sense of direction is dismal at best. I didn't want to tell my new boyfriend that I was a little unsure about where my parents *actually* lived. The second factor working against me goes hand-in-hand with the first because, when we turned into their section, I thought we were on the wrong street due to the fact that all we could see were car-lined streets. There wasn't an empty driveway or a vacant spot in front of any house to be found. Without being able to see the houses properly, I couldn't tell which house belonged to my parents! Slowly, the weight and the realization of what I was looking at washed over me.

All of these cars that took up two blocks in a rather large subdivision were there because of us! Jeff just looked at me. I had no words except, "Look, there's a place over there." He said, "It looks like someone is having a party." *Yeah. It sure does*, I thought. *Should I tell him now? Or should I wait and see what he's really made of? If I tell him now, I may need a ride back to Houston...* We started walking in the general vicinity of what I hoped to be my parents' house.

"I think all these people might be at Mom and Dad's." I tried to sound casual. He stopped walking.

"Why?" He asked, looking more than a little concerned.

"Well, I haven't brought anyone home in a long time. I'm

sure people are curious. It'll be fine. Just roll with it." I hoped he couldn't feel my hand shaking in his as we continued to get closer to the house.

When we walked inside, it was wall-to-wall people. My parents, thanks to one of my little sisters playing lookout, met us at the door. My dad shook Jeff's hand, and then proceeded to tell him everything he learned about him through the *background check* he'd obtained via the Internet that morning. He followed it with, "Hey, I needed to make sure you weren't a scumbag. She's my daughter, you know." I looked at my mother for help; she shook her head and pulled us inside. I couldn't believe the people! They were everywhere!

Turns out, no one believed I was bringing anyone home because, like I said, it had not been done in so long. Jeff did amazingly well considering he'd had a background check done on him; several Austin Police officers (they frequented the Deli *and* the restaurant) were there and wanted to ask him about his driving and criminal record; he met most of my extended family, such as grandparents and aunts and uncles; and the absolute icing on the cake was the crowd of people who wanted to know what, *exactly*, his intentions were, and if he did, in fact, plan on marrying me, was he aware that the ring he put on my finger needed to have a rock big enough to equal one carat for every child he expected me to carry for him? Ouch. It was at that point that I put a straw in a champagne bottle and sat on the couch, just waiting for the roast— I mean, the party—to be over.

Jeff handled everything in stride. He was flattered by the outpouring of people just for us, and marveled at the close-knit family relationships we shared. He didn't seem bothered at all by the great expectation imposed on him by indulgent party-goers. That *has* to be the primary difference between men and women.

Unique Family Occasions. Is it any wonder why we eloped?

The "uniqueness" didn't stop there. No. It followed us right into our married life, right on down the road...ten years down the road. You see, after my experience with the puppy backpack/leash scenario in Orlando, I decided that air travel may not be the best idea for a family of five. I did, after all, have the blessing of a monster SUV that was fully loaded with separated seats (so that no one could touch each other) and the best invention EVER for long car trips...a DVD player! We have driven to Florida two or three times...I lose count. I don't think my brain cells, unlike the cellulite cells in my thighs, are reproducing.

We have driven to California and back once. I made that trip alone with three kids: proof positive that my brain cells are dying off. We drive all over Texas, which should count as cross-country travel considering the sheer size of this state. And a couple of years ago, we drove to Kentucky. There was definitely some uniqueness working in the bluegrass of Kentucky: family. I am blessed to have (for the most part) wonderful in-laws. We all get along relatively well. They are fun and they are funny. Those are two extremely important qualities when you are spending large quantities of time with folks.

For as many times as we've crossed state lines with our children, it never ceases to amaze me that one of them will ask something really off-the-wall (at really inopportune times) in a very loud voice. For example (this is merely a detour, we will return to our Kentucky trip momentarily), Emma asked at a

Chik-Fil-A in Louisiana, "Do they speak English here?" I'm almost certain the people behind the counter did not think it was funny. I just sort of threw that one in there; even with my horrible sense of direction, I do realize that you do not have to drive through Louisiana to get to Kentucky. I digress...that was a detour for your entertainment.

We went to Kentucky for a mini family reunion on my father-in-law's side. Basically, my father-in-law wanted to get together with his three brothers, some of their kids, and us. We thought it would be a hoot, so we loaded up the kids, farmed out the dogs, and headed up to Kentucky. We kept telling the kids it was the Bluegrass state, which intrigued Emma immensely. She was forever on the hunt for *blue* grass. Therefore, because I am running for Mother of the Year, as we were driving, I would point out the window, and say, "Look Emma! Did you see it? Over there. There is blue grass in the spot over there," to which she'd reply that she hadn't, and then be disappointed until the next time, and we'd do it all over again. I can be so mean.

The boys didn't seem to care. We stayed at this sweet little cabin on a lake near Jeff's uncle's house. It was perfect for us. It had three bedrooms. The boys' room had two twin beds, Emma's room had a full-size bed, and our room had a queen size bed plus a TV. As soon as Emma saw the TV, she decided we needed to switch. The thing that blew me away the most was the price: We paid more for a hotel room in Texarkana, Texas for one night than we did for two nights in our cozy cabin by the lake in Kentucky, and it wasn't a great hotel room in Texarkana! I'm talking a one-, maybe two-star hotel. We spent most of our time with Uncle Richard and Aunt Maryann, and of course, the other brothers were there, along with my father-in-law. All of these men are fully grown, adult-type men. They should know how to behave. Wrong. They picked on each other mercilessly. This was nothing more than a case of sibling rivalry gone amuck. They told stories of the things they did to each other when they were kids, what they did as younger adults and even now, as grandpas, they continued their antics! It was a waste of time and energy to put on my makeup. They had me laughing so hard, I was crying! Then I got worried. This was in my children's DNA makeup. What in the world were my boys going to do to each other? Heaven help us.

When the conversations got to be too much for the children to handle, we took walks down the property and across the way. When you're out in the country, it's very easy to just go "across the way." It was during this trip when we discovered that Ethan is a sharpshooter. Yes. I said "sharpshooter." We come from a long line of hunters. We live in Texas. We do things like hunt for food, hunt for fun, and go to the gun range because there wasn't anything else to do last Saturday afternoon. And yes, I can say *redneck*. I *am* one. Evidently, my husband and I are raising some little rednecks as well. While my parents and my mother-in-law were busy being schooled in various areas of vehicular safety, my husband and I were busy making sure that we and our children are well-educated in gun safety.

It was during one of the talks between the grandpas that we (the next generation) decided to go "across the way" for some target practice with a couple of the cousins (because you have those, too, in the country) and some cans. We set up a two-by-four board across a couple of saw horses, stood up six cans along the board, and walked back about forty yards.

Jeff asked the kids who wanted to go first. Ethan's hand shot straight in the air. Jeff then went over some basic rules.

1. Never point a gun at anyone.
2. Always point the barrel to the ground until you are ready to shoot.
3. Always have the gun on safety until you are ready to shoot.
4. Never handle a gun unless an adult is with you.

He was answered with a resounding "Yes, sir" from Ethan after each command. Jeff loaded a little .17 caliber rifle and handed it to Ethan, who was eight at the time. Ethan took his stance, closed one eye, and fired.

BAM! One can down.

BAM! Second can down.

BAM! BAM! BAM! BAM!

He flipped the safety switch, lowered the barrel to the ground, and slowly handed the gun to his daddy. He didn't even flinch. He hit every single can. I couldn't believe it! *I* can't hit every can. This is also the same kid who has an extraordinary fascination with all military tactics and both World Wars. I see the Armed Forces in his future. Elliott didn't do quite as well; he only hit one can. I'm not 100 percent sure that the wind didn't knock that one over. Emma didn't want anything to do with that particular pastime. Turns out, she was better with a bow and arrow. She had great form, nice pull back, and great follow-through. Amazingly enough, for her size, she not only hit the target, but made the arrows stick. It's nice to know that when the world ends, we won't starve. Each one of us brings a little something new and exciting to the table...literally. We each actually have the ability to bring something to the table. Only trouble: I'm the only one who knows how to cook it.

Jeff & Ethan getting ready for a little target practice in the hills of Kentucky, 2009.

Emma with Cousin Randy, getting her bow and arrow lined up correctly. Kentucky, 2009.

Unique Family Occasions. Alien adventures. Close encounters of the third kind...

There's another member of our family that I've not introduced you to. His name is Nelson. Nelson is very special to us. In fact, rarely do we travel anywhere without him. There are times when we leave him behind. For instance, we did not take Nelson to Kentucky, but most of the time, particularly when we are traveling in and around Texas, Nelson is our favorite companion; he is our travel trailer. When I married into this family, I knew they were fairly "outdoorsy." Jeff's step-dad was a huge proponent of camping; me, not so much. Little did I know that the type of camping Papa Jim did would be redneck luxury at its finest! (It was Papa Jim who introduced us to our Nelson.)

Papa Jim & Ethan
May, 2003

Perhaps you've heard the saying that everything is bigger in Texas. Well, truer words have never been spoken, especially when referring to Nelson; he is a little more than forty feet long. He has two bedrooms and two bathrooms, one kitchen, a dining area, and a living room big enough for a full-size sleeper sofa. Anything that big needed a name. We listen to a lot of country music where I come from, and one of my all-time favorites, really one of the all-time greats of country music, is Willie Nelson. His song *On the Road Again* is the anthem for gypsies everywhere. I didn't want to name this beast Willie...but Nelson had a nice ring to it. Voila! He had his name.

We've been everywhere in Nelson. We could live in Nelson if we needed to. Our fondest memories are during hunting season, not because we all ride around on four-wheelers with shotguns just looking for defenseless animals to shoot at, but because of the fellowship that takes place between each and every member of my family and the friends that go with us. When we are out on our property, we are just that—out. There are no Internet connections. There isn't any cable TV. No satellite. The kids play outside with rocks and sticks and make forts out of cedar tree branches. Then their allergies bother them for a week, but the point is that they had a blast.

They hike up the hills and go in search of any nests where the deer might be bedded down during the day. They look for tracks. They learn how to scope out mesquite trees looking for "rubs" or places where bucks are rubbing the velvet off their antlers. Being out and about as a family cements us together. There are few distractions in the hill country. There isn't a Wii gaming console, even though we could hook one up, if we so chose to. The kids learn how to build fires, *real* fires. They've also learned that fires burn hot.

Living in the city has effectively muted our basic survival skills. We've somehow gotten away from the thrill and the joy of being able to do things ourselves and with our own two hands because we've come to be incredibly dependent on the conveniences of modern technology. Don't get me wrong, I love modern technology! I think TiVo is fantastic. It's like it *knows* what I want to watch. I enjoy a pedicure just like any other woman. I get my nails done every two weeks. I have to have some girlie vices. But I believe it is imperative that we teach our children how to be outside. We have to teach them that there is more to life than the latest video game, or more than the latest new pair of shoes.

There is a whole other world waiting to be discovered. That world includes Nanas who ride great big motorcycles and Grannies who drive huge, red, big rig trucks. That world is full of dirt and fast-moving creeks. Kids need to be shown the difference between pets and wildlife; between snakes that simply slither and snakes that will land you in the ER. This parenting thing is an adventure. Parenting is the final frontier. We will be faced with aliens from other worlds disguised as sweet innocents (a.k.a., our children). We will have close encounters of a third kind (a.k.a., our in-laws). But through all of that, if we stick together, we will survive...

Granny, Papaw and Ethan, May 2003

Jeff and the kids at Granny and Papaw's house in Austin.

It's Fun to Feed a Fish

· ·

I haven't really made it a secret that I come from the south... Actually, I come from the west, *and* the south, which lands me right smack-dab into a whole new category of stereotypes. Down here in Texas, one of our most favorite things in all the world is duct tape. For the longest time, I thought the word was "duck" tape, as in *quack-quack*, until someone explained that it was actually *duct*, as in an air conditioning duct... Oh, the things we learn!

At any rate, down here, we use this stuff for everything. It's wonderful! We make school projects out of it. We can fix broken windows with it. We can even duct tape a car bumper to hold it in place, as made evident by one of my neighbors... I did mention the new stereotype class I'd just put myself in, right? Lately, I've noticed that not only does it come in your classic silver, but manufacturers have wised up and discovered that the female population has realized what a unique, diverse, and useful little find this roll of ingenuity can really be, thus making it available in fashion-friendly designs. You can pick up the ever-popular roll of duct tape in hot pink, bright red, basic black, and even camo green or camo pink. Google duct tape prom dresses, and I promise your mouth will drop wide open, and then you will need your own roll of duct tape in order to get it closed again. Why am I telling you all of this? There are lots of uses for duct tape. We've already walked through the scenario of using leashes (some call them backpacks) on our kids. I have a very sarcastic sense of humor, and I may have said in the past that all you really need in order to raise good and obedient kids are leashes and duct tape. Folks, I was kidding.

Although duct tape has some excellent and creative uses, child restraint is not one of them. On February 17, 2011, a San Bernardino County, California woman (Danyella Higgins) was arrested for endangering a child (*her* two-year-old child) when she duct taped the child's hands, feet, and mouth, *took a picture* of the child, and then sent the picture via text message to a friend. The friend quickly called authorities, who were then dispatched to the woman's house. They found the child relatively unharmed (except for trace pieces of duct tape still clinging to various body parts) and the nineteen-year-old mother spluttering excuses about taping up a window, and then thinking it would be funny to use duct tape on the baby. The child was removed immediately from her and placed in Child Protective Services custody.[1]

Do you see anything wrong with this picture? I see several things. During this chapter, we will take a look at them all, and probably follow a few rabbit trails along the way. The obvious and screaming question is: *WHO DUCT TAPES THEIR KID?!* Don't you know that is wrong?! The best answer that I can come up with is: No, perhaps she didn't. The mother in question was nineteen years old. She's not much more than a baby herself. Chances are no one has ever told her that duct taping your baby is wrong. It sounds very trivial to you and to me, but sometimes that's what it boils down to.

Think about this for a minute: How did you learn to tie your shoes? Someone had to show you. Someone had to sit you down and teach you how to loop, swoop, and pull. Parenting is the same way. For anyone reading this book right now who has never been told: Please DO NOT duct tape your kids. I will help you discipline your kids with more humanity, whilst also leaving your sanity intact.

I will also give you another little disclaimer: I have an "old school" background, but please don't let that scare you. Keep reading—if for no other reason than your own entertainment. Here we go.

Close to our house is one of those behemoth pet stores. You know the kind. It's bigger than two football fields and smells twice as bad as three locker rooms combined. You walk through the automatic sliding doors and your ears are instantly assaulted with the screeches and cries of the caged birds and the spinning wheels of the rat-cousins (better known as "hamsters").

My children and I entered this Utopia one afternoon. We were there to buy dog food. I typically don't bring my children to the pet store. The temptations are too strong. It's like the Jedi Force drawing them closer and closer to the kennels where the ferrets are kept or the aquariums where the reptiles slither... They just can't help themselves. Apparently, on this particular day, the Force was working on me, too, because when they wanted to go look at the fish, I consented. We left the pet store that day with our thirty-five-pound sack of dog food and a four-ounce shaker of fish food. The kids had convinced me that our life simply would not be complete without this: the prettiest of little blue fish. Of course, a fish needs a bowl, and some fake marine plant life, and a castle to swim in and out of, and finally, some rocks to go on the bottom of the bowl. Home we went with Flippy secure in Ethan's hands, and the other two kids each holding on to something equally treasured, so as to feel included in the arrival of Flippy to our house. Have you ever had a fish? Flippy was our first fish as a family. I knew the basic knowledge of how to care for fish, but anything beyond that, we would have to learn as we went.

For starters, I knew that for Flippy's utter well-being, he/she (still not sure what it was—boy or girl) absolutely had to stay in his bowl. That fact was undeniable. Even though we felt sorry for Flippy stuck swimming around and around and around, looking at the same view over and over and over again, his bowl provided the necessary habitat that was life-sustaining for him. Outside of his bowl, he would most certainly die. We moved his bowl from time to time, trying to give him new things to look at, but taking Flippy out of his bowl was out of the question.

Something else I knew about fish was their food. It's fun to feed a fish. Their food looks like powder. When you shake it from the box, it floats gently and gracefully down to the surface of the water and hovers there for just a brief moment until Flippy comes stealthily from underneath to snatch it! It doesn't matter how much food or how many times in a day you feed Flippy, he will always eat. This is a highly amusing past time for children...highly amusing and entertaining for children, but lethal for poor Flippy. We set up a schedule of turns for which child could feed Flippy, trying to avoid the unavoidable. This worked for awhile. However, over time, the Force was too strong, and the children's resistance was no match, Flippy's food proved to be too great a temptation... Flippy was the permanent Guest of Honor at a Las-Vegas-style, all-you-can-eat buffet. It was a sad, sad day. Flippy quite literally ate himself to death. Why? How? Well, it's fun to feed a fish. But, it's not always the best thing for them. They need boundaries; they need rules. It's the same with children.

• • • • • •

Children need the same safety and security given to them that is afforded to a fish in its bowl of water. Now, I'm not suggesting you stick your child in a bowl full of water, but hear me out on this. Children need boundaries. Boundaries keep them safe. Without boundaries, kids wander off, they stray too far, they get into unfamiliar territory, and they find themselves unable to breathe. With all of that said, when our kids were babies, we did the appropriate baby-proofing of the house. We installed magnetic tot-locks on all the kitchen cabinets. Looking back, we could've just put them on the cabinet that held the cleaners. We had plastic outlet covers on every single outlet in the house. Those worked great until the kids figured out how to take them off. Amazingly enough, no one has been electrocuted yet. The best investment in child safety we ever made were the gates at the top and bottom of the stairs.

Aside from those adjustments to the house, everything

else stayed the same. The house still belonged to my husband and to myself. The kids were an added bonus. We didn't want to be one of those couples who'd lost the ability to relate to other people simply because we now had a baby (or two or three). Granted, our living room floor did closely resemble the show room of FAO Schwartz for a while, but that was to be expected. Three babies in two years will effectively rearrange your living room. However, the basic structure of the house didn't change. Of course, giving your child these "boundaries" will most assuredly not win you any popularity contests *at first*, but they will pay off in the end.

Because my kids were babies all at the same time, it seemed like the first word they were going to say would be "no." It was all I said. Each time one of them would crawl to the stairs, "No-no." The dog food bowl was their absolute favorite hangout... but that was always followed with "No-no" from me because while dog food is delicious, it is truly only nutritious for dogs, not babies...even though they did eat plenty of it until they figured out it doesn't taste very good. The dogs' water bowl was another favorite haunt. Many a Weeble wobbled and drowned in the dogs' water bowl. My pictures on low-lying shelves were under constant attack from the kids. Still, the pictures stayed where they were. I didn't move them.

The one item in the house that drew those kids to it just like ants at a picnic was my cuckoo clock that my parents brought back to me from Germany. Cuckoo clocks have L-O-N-G chains that hang down, so the clock itself needs to be hung at least six feet off the ground so the chains have room to move. It's the movement of these chains that actually wind the clock and keep the sweet little cuckoo bird, well, cuckooing. Let's pause right here for a moment and explore some of my options:

- Option one: Take the clock off the wall instead of having to deal with the constant threat of three kids tugging on the chains. (Okay, I could do that.)
- Option two: Move the clock to a more secure location; this way it's not put away, per se, but it is safer.
- Option three: Teach these little tricycle motors that this is my house, with my things in it, and they have plenty of their own stuff to touch, eat, and destroy. They do not need to lay their chubby fingers (even though they are incredibly cute, chubby fingers) on my cuckoo clock.

I went with option three, and let me tell you why: If our house was the only house my children ever went to, I'd be happy to move everything out of their reach. But that isn't realistic. I have friends. I have friends who do not yet have children. I would like to be able to take my children with me when I visit their house, and better yet, after visiting their houses once with my kids—I'd like to be invited back. We cannot move everything in our houses up four feet off the ground so that Junior cannot reach it until he's three. Know why? Because by the time he's three, he will think *he* owns the house, not the other way around. This is the same reason I always decorated ALL of my Christmas tree. *Yes, the tree is beautiful. Yes, it is lovely. Oh! I know you want to touch it, but we mustn't because it isn't safe.*

Kids are smart. Tell Junior that climbing to the top of

the Christmas tree is unsafe. Use some common sense with priceless family heirlooms. Ornaments that have been passed down from your great, great, great grandmother may want to either wait for a later date or be placed near the *top* of the tree. I have my grandmother's nativity scene. To me, it is priceless. My kids are somewhat passed the "I-want-to-touch-every-thing" stage, and I *still* put that set where no one can reach it. Why? Because I would be heartbroken if something happened to it. My grandmother is gone. Sometimes there is a legitimate reason why we tell them "no." Sometimes it's for their own safety. Sometimes, the answer is "no" simply because we said so. Either way, you're the parent. Stand your ground.

. . . . . .

Children are among the smartest criminals...I mean *people*... on the planet. And it starts from an extremely young age. No one has to teach them how to manipulate a situation. It seems to be already installed into their hard-wiring. It's amazing to watch, but mortifying to live through. Allow me to share a page from my Most Embarrassing Moments Scrapbook.

When Ethan was about nine months old, my Colorado in-laws came to visit. You haven't met them, yet. Dan and Linda are some of the sweetest people in the world, very laid back, and incredibly non-confrontational. At this point in time, I was already pretty pregnant with Emma, so between hormones and throwing everything up...my fuse was a little short. Can you see where the drama might have room to grow? Any time you decide to take a nine-month-old child out to eat in public, you run the risk of a nuclear core meltdown—either from the child, one or both parents, or the restaurant staff. During this night out, the meltdown that occurred involved all of the above. Please hold your applause until the end.

At nine months old, Ethan was filled to over-flowing with the wiggles. He couldn't sit still for longer than a few minutes at any given time. This is not unusual for most babies. However, dealing with said wiggles is a learning experience for both baby and parents. This is one of the hardest parts of parenting—BAR NONE. You see, Ethan wanted out of his highchair. I wasn't going to hold him, Jeff wasn't going to hold him, and even though his grandparents would've held him, this wasn't a viable option. Why? Because we, as the parents, wanted to take this opportunity to teach Ethan that we were in control of the situation, not *him*. He tried to climb out of the highchair; we used the seat belts and strapped him in. He was thrilled—NOT! He began to cry. His grandmother tried to appease him with bread. The kid could have medaled for gold in the shot-put event in the next Olympics, with the distance he put on the rolls he chunked across the restaurant. I dug into the magic and normally bottomless diaper bag for more tricks. He was not interested. Toy after toy after cup after the ultimate weapon—the bottle—which landed on the floor. I picked it up, and handed it back to him. He threw it again, and it landed behind us. I picked it up one more—and final—time. For the grand finale, he threw the bottle on the table beside us.

Ethan's cries began to escalate into screams. For those of you who have not yet experienced this ratchet up the volume scale, just wait. There is a substantial difference between a crying baby and a screaming baby. Enter the manager of the restaurant. Ethan now has his back in a full arch, arms flailing, face beet-red, fighting with everything in him against the restraints keeping him in the wooden chair, while his father politely cuts the rest of the chicken on his own plate as though nothing is going nuclear beside him. My in-laws are averting their eyes from the scene. I'm suggesting that maybe we should just leave, when the manager says, "Is there anything I can do to help?" Jeff just looked up at him, smiled, and said, "I could use some more tea. Thanks for stopping by."

Have you ever had that dream where you're walking down the street naked? And everyone can see you? Yeah. That's where I was at that moment. Jeff was proving a point. There was a battle of wills taking place between Ethan and Jeff. It boiled down to who had the biggest stubborn streak. Turns out, my husband does. That highchair represented everything Ethan hated about life on that day. He didn't want to be restrained. He wanted to be free to roam, to play, to dump all the salt on the table, and pull all the little packets of sugar out of their basket. He wanted to sit in the middle of the table and kick his legs and laugh and coo at everyone in the place. Was there anything so wrong with that?

Well, yes, as a matter of fact. For starters, children don't belong on the table. They belong in chairs. Secondly, I mentioned boundaries being set in place for children's own good and safety; well, what I haven't told you is *where* we were having dinner. We were eating at a place called Texas Land & Cattle Company; it's a steak house. This place literally has the biggest steak knives I've ever seen in my life. Had we let Ethan out of his chair, even if one of us were holding him, he would've been within range of one of those knives. It was for his safety and wellbeing that he remained in his chair. Then, there's the old standby that just so happens to be my favorite: He needed to be in his chair because that's where we put him, and because we said so.

That little trip out to eat was one of the most brutal trips to a restaurant that I've ever had to endure. It honestly was. But, you know something? It only took that one time. The next time we went out to eat, he stayed in his chair. Kids not only need boundaries, they *want* them. We live in a society today that is so utterly confused about the role of the parent, it astounds me. I love my children so much it actually hurts sometimes. I'm filled to the point of overwhelming emotion when I watch them sleep, when I listen to them actually being sweet to each other, or watch them participate in school programs.

I spent this very afternoon playing *Fish Out of Water* with them on the playground of the elementary school around the corner from our house. We had a blast! My husband was tagged twice. Even through all of those emotions and fun times, our primary role in their life is one of authority over them. It is not our job to be their *friend*, it is our job to be their *parent*. There is a big difference between the two. Parenting is not for sissies. It requires strength you never knew you had. You will undergo on-the-job mind-training worthy of Jedi fighters. You will learn how to function on less sleep than prisoners of war in a concentration camp. You will discover that consistency is your secret weapon and it is the key to winning not only the battle, but the entire war. The goal is to raise up good and decent, functioning adults. We want to raise our kids to grow into adulthood so they can leave our homes, and go into the world to become productive citizens. They will need basic skill sets in order to do this. They need a solid foundation of right and wrong and consequences for their wrong choice and/or actions. They need an understanding and a healthy respect for those in authority over them.

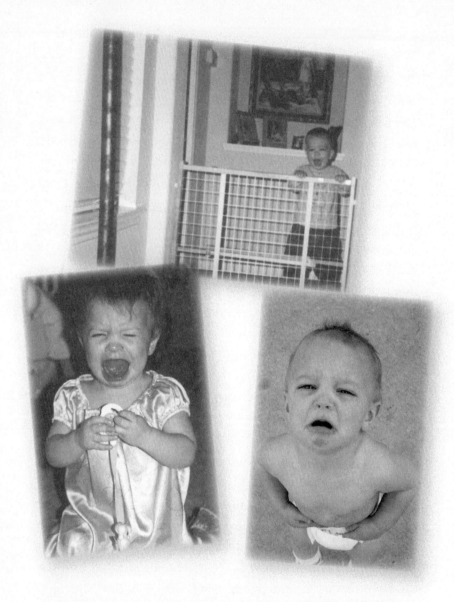

At some point in time, all of the children had their own idea about how I should discipline them. Can you guess who won?

• • • • • •

We live in a two-story house. The house is about twelve years old. When it was built, apparently open floor plans were all the rage. We have a large playroom/game room directly over the downstairs living room. You can hear everything that goes on upstairs. I can hear my boys drop a Lego. My staircase is off to one side of my living room; up the side of the staircase is a wall lined with framed pictures of the family. My pictures line the wall from the railing to as far up as I can reach. I have three very strong-willed children. I love their strong wills and their spirits and their spunk...most of the time. However, it makes parenting these types of children a challenge. I have to be able to discipline them effectively without breaking their spirits. I want them to know that I mean business, but I cannot do this by means of bullying them, scaring them, or beating them into submission. Neat trick, right?

My daughter is exceedingly dramatic. Everything is a monumental deal. So, each time she gets mad, or has her feelings hurt, she *stomps* up the stairs. Emma is a petite, little thing. You'd think this wouldn't be a problem. Dynamite is little, too, and we all know what dynamite can do! As she *stomps* deliberately up each individual step, every picture on my wall rattles so terribly I think it will come crashing down at any moment. This is not a new tactic for Emma. And the consequence that follows is not new either, even though she acts like it is. I will wait until she gets to the top of the stairs, and call her back down. STOMP—STOMP—STOMP... She doesn't say anything; she just looks at me. This, too, is unacceptable behavior. So, we wait in an Old West-style, duel stand-off.

She's often the first to cave at speaking, "Ma'am?" (I told y'all being from the south *and* the west sticks me into a completely different stereotypical category. We say "ma'am" and "sir" down here.) I remind her that her way of pounding up and down my stairs is not the passable way of doing it. Therefore, she needs to do it again. Typically, I get mouth, lip, attitude...whatever you want to call it. In the end, I get my way, and back up she goes...usually a couple of times, because the first time or two she is still fairly peeved at the thought of having to walk up and down the stairs again.

Here's where the consistency pays off. Having her walk back up the stairs one time isn't going to do the trick if she stomps up the stairs on her do-over. She has to walk up the stairs as many times as it takes until she can walk up the stairs without rattling the pictures on my walls. It goes back to respect. Does she respect me enough to listen to what I'm telling her? If those pictures fall, I'm the one who has to clean up the mess and replace the frame and re-hang it. She needs to understand that simply because she's upset about something does not give her the right to destroy the property that belongs to someone else.

After she completes her task of walking up the stairs and goes to her room for whatever reason, then I'll go up and sit with her to reassure her that I love her, and we'll talk through what's bothering her. Whatever the discipline, the bottom line is the love behind it. It's easy to give them what they want. It's easy to be the fun parent all the time. It's easy to mistake that for love. Love is actually keeping them safe. Remember: A fish out of water won't be able to breathe.

It boils down to respect, and respect is a big deal at our house. I think that's a big deal everywhere, although from my vantage point, lack of respect seems to be a better fit. Kids, and especially older kids and teenagers, have little to no respect for others or other people's property. My children have been guilty of this at times, too.

So, a couple of months ago I get a phone call from Elliott's teacher. I love getting these phone calls in the middle of the day. I can handle phone calls from the nurse. Those mean someone is sick or hurt, as you will see in later chapters. A phone call from the teacher—that's a different matter entirely. Elliott is my baby. He's the youngest. He's probably one of the brightest kids I know (intellect-wise, although I would never tell him that—it would make his head swell), and most of the time he's the sweetest of my three kiddos. So, when his teacher called to tell me he'd just come from a little visit to the principal's office for behavior, needless to say, I was stunned into silence.

Once I found my voice, I asked her if she was sure it was Elliott. She laughed and assured me that she had indeed sent the right child to the office. I wanted to know what he had done, because going to the office was no small feat. Here's the deal: He'd been busted for throwing wet paper towels up against the bathroom wall and watching them stick during a bathroom break. Honestly, I was relieved it wasn't something worse. She said he was downright devastated at having to go to the office. I'm sure he was. I promised her that he would be reprimanded at home; after all, it had been some time since we'd been able to use the hot pokers or the rack. She laughed again, thanked me, and finished with, "Just thought you'd want to know." Boy, did I ever.

I'm totally sure that throwing wet paper towels up against the bathroom wall was great fun during a bathroom break, especially knowing your teacher is a *girl* and cannot come into the *boys* bathroom. Safe bet for some free playtime, right? Wrong. The vice principal's office (who just so happens to be a boy) is next door to said bathroom. Oops. Seven-year-olds don't think about that. I told you I come from an "old school" background, which means that I got spanked growing up. I'm a firm believer that a swat on the backside makes a child's ears open up.

I spent a great deal of time with my great-grandmother when I was a kid. As a matter of fact, when I was about Elliott's age, she had a paddle that she named, "Put Me to Work." I'm familiar with spankings, as are my kids. However, the punishment needs to fit the crime. I didn't figure taking a page out of Mamaw's book was the best plan right now. So, I thought I'd show Elliott the "proper" way to use a paper towel. That afternoon, after school, he cleaned the upstairs bathroom. He wiped down the counter and cleaned the mirror. He complained the entire time. I stood right beside him, letting him know, "You missed a spot." I'd grin, and when I was comfortable with the state of the bathroom, I had him sit down and write his teacher a letter, apologizing for his behavior, signed with the promise that he will never do it again. He has not had to clean the upstairs bathroom again. But, Ethan...well that's another story...

We are blessed enough to have a service come and clean the house every other week. I love Wednesdays. My house smells so good. My floors feel good. On two Wednesdays a month, you cannot tell that three kids and two dogs live here. It's a gift from heaven. But then, we come home from school, and life takes over, and it's Wednesday night and you can't tell the cleaning girls were ever here.

A couple of weeks ago, on a Wednesday, my girls came to the house. They worked their magic and life was good. All three kids' rooms are upstairs. They all three share one bathroom upstairs, even though there are two up there. This, come to think of it, is probably a good thing, because then I'd have two bathrooms to clean every other week instead of the one. It just so happens that the kids had been sick—not bad sick—congested sick, coughing, runny noses, etc. I had been running vaporizers in their rooms at night to help with the coughing. As I was putting them to bed recently, I began to refill the vaporizers. In order to assure that you have the best possible steam, you must empty the old water and put the new water in. I carried the first machine to the bathtub and was about to pour the old water into the bathtub when I looked in the tub and found the biggest mess I'd seen in quite some time. Someone had squirted hair conditioner up the wall, in the tub, and all across half of the tub. From the looks of the mess, the culprit had been sitting on the potty and the conditioner (that I buy in a pump dispenser for Emma) was still sitting in the corner of the tub.

It was time for a family meeting in the bathroom. Someone needed to be held accountable for the fresh mess. I called all three kids into the bathroom, pointed to the tub, and just said, "Well?" I received one, "Not me." One said, "Oh, gross!" and the last one, eyes averted, was looking anywhere but the tub or at me. There was my offender. I just love my Mommy Radar. It comes standard with every positive pregnancy test. You *do* get to upgrade the frequency of your Mommy Radar Operating System for free with every kid and every birthday your oldest kiddo has. New operating systems come out each year. Right now, I'm working off of MROS-9.

"Uh, Ethan, is there anything you want to tell me?" The other two seemed to be glued to the spots where they stood; I think they would've been passing out popcorn to each other if they'd had any. But, I cut their fun short, "You two can go. Ethan?" Emma and Elliott moved toward the door, but said under their breath, "How does she *know*?" Turns out, he was, in fact, sitting on his throne, and he was bored. Guess I should start putting his Lego magazines in there. He told me he pushed the pump just "to see what it would do." I said, "For starters, it's a *pump*, so I'm guessing it was going to pump." He said, "Yeah, it did. And I thought it was cool. So, I pushed it again and again and again. Then I kinda made a mess."

His plan was to clean it up when he took a shower that night, but surprise! No shower that night. Once again, I thought of my grandmother's paddle. I needed to pick my battles strategically, and conditioner in the bathtub was not a hill to die on. Instead, I told him to go downstairs and ask Daddy for the Comet bathroom cleaner and a clean rag. Then, my honor roll student looked at me and asked, "Why?" I just smiled.

He came back upstairs and I proceeded to explain to him how to clean a bathtub. I was somewhat put-out because my cleaning girls had just been there. Again, this discipline thing goes back to a safety issue. Conditioner is slippery. The first kid to climb into that bathtub would've busted their little tooshie. I'm much more interested in my children's character than head stitches due to someone's noggin hitting the faucet.

I made him rinse the conditioner out of the tub. He said "Finished," and made like he was going to leave the bathroom. Wrong again, chief. I showed him how to sprinkle the powder, and was immediately met with, "OH MY GOODNESS THIS SMELLS TERRIBLE. MOM, SERIOUSLY (gasp, cough, choke). (Apparently Emma isn't the only one with mad drama skills.) I—CAN'T—B-R-E-A-T-H-E." Then, as he was left with no option but to complete the cleanup, he would turn his head away from the tub, take a big breath, and then get back to work wiping out the inside of the tub. "MOM (gasp, choke, cough), HOW MUCH LONGER?" I showed him how to rinse, trying so hard not to laugh. "MOM, REALLY. WHY ARE YOU MAKING (cough, gasp) ME DO THIS? DIDN'T THE GIRLS JUST COME?"

Thank you, son. It was the perfect opportunity to explain to him that, yes, my girls *had* just come, but he'd chosen to ruin the work they'd just done. This foul smelling cleaner (which doesn't smell that bad), that he can't stand, is what they had just cleaned this bathtub with. He carelessly chose to squirt conditioner all over the tub, thus making it unsafe for anyone to get into because of the slipperiness of the conditioner. This was a boundary I was setting for him. One he won't soon forget. Kids need boundaries.

Have you ever seen those antiquated, wire-and-pole electric fences used in backyards for puppies? No, I'm not suggesting that you use electric fences on your kids. (Can't you see the headlines now as a direct result of this book?: "Woman Tells Readers to Use Duct Tape and Electric Fences for Discipline!" Good grief! Stay with me for a minute while I make my point.) With an electric fence, a puppy or even a grown dog will test its boundaries every now and then to see if there are any weak spots. They won't do it all the time, and not every day; just from time to time. It's the same with kids and their boundaries.

I have great kids. They are obedient, contrary to the last couple of stories. I can send them to their friends' houses for dinners and sleepovers and know that when I get them back, I will hear about their manners and good behavior. But every now and then, they test their "fence." When kids do this, you must be ready with your follow-through! Do not spout empty threats. If you say you are going to do something—think like Nike, and JUST DO IT! They know when you are bluffing.

Case in point: Two years ago, we found ourselves at Disney World again for Spring Break. (Apparently, we didn't learn the first time we were there with the multitudes.) This time, we drove—and this time, we were *sans babysitter*. The kids were older and we thought we could handle it. (Famous last words...) The parks had more people in them than I ever thought possible. I Googled "max attendance" just to get a ballpark figure. I swear the max attendance was off by at least twenty-five thousand. Wall-to-wall people, and us right in the middle. Since we'd been there before, the kids had their own ideas about which ride to go on next, and how to use the FastPass, and above anything else, how boring Mom and Dad were. Well, I get a little nervous when I'm stuck in the middle of a crowd of close to one hundred thousand people, and my kids keep running in three different directions. I had just about had enough of Ethan and Elliott bolting from me when I corralled them all and shouted above the noise of everyone else, "If anyone else runs away from me, I'm calling the hotel and getting a sitter for y'all, and Daddy and I will come back to Disney without you!" Ethan defiantly looked me square in the eye and said, "You would not." I stood straight up, and said, "Try me."

Ten minutes later, he was gone again. He wanted to do

Splash Mountain, and none of us were all that fired up about getting wet again, so we said no, to which he didn't really care. The only real problem with our decision was, I didn't know which direction he'd gone. Splash Mountain was one way at a fork, and we were headed down the other side. It took a long minute to find him. I was close to being panicked by the time we got reunited with him. That probably would've taught him a lesson, too, because we'd been separated long enough to scare him. The only trouble with leaving it at that lesson was that I'd told all three kids that if anyone ran off again, I was getting them a sitter. Ethan ran off, and I called the hotel. Jeff's jaw literally hit the ground. He couldn't believe I actually did that.

Our hotel is part of one of the largest and best-known hotel chains in the world...five stars, and the whole nine yards. My thinking behind this was that we couldn't be the only parents who needed a slight break from their kids. Turns out, we weren't. They had a Mary Poppins wannabe ready for us in a matter of hours. We left the park and headed back to our hotel. The kids sat in stunned silence all the way back. Although it was Ethan's choice to run toward Splash Mountain that broke the proverbial camel's back, all three children were guilty of unsupervised excursions through the Magic Kingdom. My decision to return all of them to the hotel was justified for all three. This is all about the follow-through. I laid some ground rules that if a certain action happened again, there would be an opposite and swift reaction from me. The children apparently didn't believe me; therefore, they tested the strength of their electric fence. They did not find a weak spot. Instead, they found all circuits fully functional and wired hot.

(On a side note: The woman the hotel sent to us was, in

fact, Mary Poppins' double. She had a bag full of tricks, complete with games, crafts, and who knows what else! When we got back to the hotel that night, the kitchen counter was lined with twenty or so pictures and crafts that the children had made. I guess I should've told her she was a *punishment*! The next morning, the kids asked when Miss Betty could come back.)

I realize that we mix and match things from our past with things from our present in order to try to make our lives make sense for our future. I mean, I raise my kids mostly based on the way that I was raised. My parents and my extended family did a good job with me. My husband has the same train of thought. Together, we are on the same page. These pieces of information are not just important when raising your children—they are vital to the overall health of your children and the health of your family, and critical to the survival of your marriage. Very few things will drive a wedge further and faster between a husband and wife than that of disagreements on how to discipline your children.

I remember Jeff and I sitting and talking about seemingly little things before we got married. We would laugh and joke about getting grounded when we were kids. We discussed whether or not we got spanked, to which we both replied, "Yep." We both had similar experiences with school versus home. When we got in trouble at school, there was going to be more waiting at home. Remembering these things made us both smile. Not because we are gluttons for punishment. Our parents didn't beat us. We were not abused children. Our parents knew what was going on in our world. My mother talked to my teachers. She was involved. I'm the oldest of four girls. Mother *had* to be involved. Jeff's folks did the same thing. I understand that for some of you reading this book, you and your spouse come from different backgrounds. That does make things a bit more challenging... It makes things *challenging*; it *doesn't* make them impossible.

When two people get married, they get to start fresh. They leave their parents' house and cleave to each other. That means they stick together. When you get married, you begin to form your own new family unit with new family traditions, new rules, and a new game plan. You don't discount the way you were brought up, you simply weave from your past, *both* of your pasts, into your future. Everyone will have something new to tell you and some new way for you to do things. Look at me! What do you think I'm doing? I'm telling you what has worked for us. This can work for you, too, as it has for us... most days. (Not every day, but most days!) My kids, cute as they are, are still kids. And they will be the first to tell you, it's super fun to feed a fish, but when you feed Flippy too much, he explodes.

Me & the kids
June, 2009

You Shoved *What* Up Your Nose?

We want our kid to grow up to be a doctor,
but instead he grows up needing a doctor.
—Tom Bergeron

Having kids running in and around and through your house will inevitably cause one of them to explode every now and again. Hopefully, these explosions will be minor, thus only causing you to pull some frozen peas from the freezer or perhaps send you to visit your local pharmacy or pediatrician. But once in a while, kids will pull a stunt worthy of Evel Knievel himself, which will require an emergency stop into a specialist's office or the Mother Ship, a.k.a., the Emergency Room. Throughout the course of this book, you've become fairly well-acquainted with my three children (hopefully). Would you believe at the time of printing, we've not had *any* broken bones?

I probably just jinxed myself.

Oh, don't worry! We've had plenty of other fun ailments, we just haven't yet had the pleasure of resetting any bones... A nose doesn't really count as a bone, does it?

(As the story goes, I spoke too soon! Please see the end of this chapter for the addendum to this last claim!)

Do you remember the TV show, *Everybody Loves Raymond*? Well, contrary to popular belief, not everybody really does love Raymond. I happen to love Raymond, well, Marie (Ray's mom) actually, but my children don't love anyone from the show. In fact, when we go surfing through the channels and I happen to land on *Raymond*, the moans and wails that come spouting from my children can only be compared to the wailing and gnashing of teeth one might hope to find at the End of Days (biblically speaking). "Not Raymond! I don't *love* Raymond!" And so on and so forth. Why am I telling you this?

My mind is circling around one particular episode in which Marie is showcasing her abilities as a human thermometer. I got the biggest kick out of this episode. Marie can tell by touch if someone has a fever, and if so, what that fever is—down to the decimal. She does this by kissing the person's forehead. It just so happens to be Debra, Ray's wife, who comes down with the fever, so she is the recipient of Marie's red lipstick lip-prints all over her forehead. This is an ability that has been given to mothers everywhere. It utterly astounds my husband.

When I began writing this book, I was on a west-bound plane headed to California for some much-needed rest and relaxation. I left all three of my children in the care of their father (my husband). I was comfortable in my decision not to call in the cavalry (my mother-in-law). I felt sure that he was competent enough to handle the homework, the lunches, the bedtimes, the breakfasts, and even the dinners. I had high hopes that teeth would be brushed a couple of times over the course of the week that I would be gone, and that baths would also be administered at least twice over the course of seven days. What I did not count on was a phone call from my daughter four days into my trip. This is where you re-think teaching your children your cell phone number. Here's what our conversation sounded like:

Me: Hello?

Emma: Mom? When are you coming home?

Me: Not for a few more days. Why? Is everything okay? Where's Daddy?

Emma: He's in his office. We don't feel very good.

Me: (Stomach does a back flip.) What do you mean "we"? Where are your brothers? What doesn't feel good?

Emma: The boys are here. We are coughing. And we feel... we just don't...feel...good.

Me: What does Daddy say?

Emma: He said we were fine. We needed to go to bed and go to sleep.

Me: Put Daddy on the phone.

Now, from California, there wasn't an awful lot I could do. I couldn't lean over and kiss them to see who had fever and who didn't. I couldn't listen effectively to their cough to discern who needed the doctor and who needed a Benadryl. My husband, bless his heart, comes from the school of thought that eventually your body will heal itself. And when you're forty, perhaps that works. But, when you're a little kid...I'm not buying it. I came home from California three days later to three kids with sinus infections, two kids with bronchitis, and one with croup. Ten days worth of antibiotics later and all three are right as rain. (Mom Radar...there's a reason why we are the moms. MROS-9... Upgrade yours today!)

I didn't always have the latest version of the Mom Radar. Lucky for me, my kids have always tested me on whichever version I was running though. My boys have asthmatic tendencies. That means they don't have full-blown asthma, but when they do get something like bronchitis, they wheeze with gusto. This set of symptoms has caused us to purchase our very own nebulizer machine so we can administer breathing treatments whenever they are needed. When the boys were babies, this happened ALL THE TIME. It seemed they were constantly sick. Then I kept adding a new kid to the mix every year, so I was at the doctor every other week for something. I was there for shots for one kid, sick visit for another, or an ear re-check for still another one. It was during one of these visits when my pediatrician mentioned to me that she thought both Ethan and Emma would benefit greatly from having ear tubes put in. Emma was six months old and Ethan was twenty months old, and I was pregnant with Elliott. Between the both of them, we'd had seventeen ear infections in the house. It was time for tubes.

She recommended a wonderful ear, nose, and throat doctor and one week later the surgery was scheduled. Little did we know, I wouldn't be able to make that surgery. The day after scheduling their surgery, I was put in a different hospital due to extreme dehydration. My doctor kept me there for a week and some change. Jeff had to handle the ear tube surgery without me.

Now, before y'all get too worried about him, he had *his* momma with him. Nana wasn't about to let him fly completely solo on this gig. She was there to do the heavy lifting. Besides, those babies came out of anesthesia fighting like tigers, from what I understand, and Nana was the only one that could've controlled them anyway! There's a magical peace that comes from the arms of the Nanas and the Grannies. Maybe it's because they've already lived through this. Maybe it's because they know they get to give these fighting kids back to their parents and then walk away. Who knows? All I *do* know is that on that day, we could not have done this without her. Thankfully, the tubes worked like a charm, and the ear infections disappeared. Sweet as our Dr. Chan was, and as well as the tubes worked, that would not be the last we were to see of him.

I'm a firm believer that children are really just super cute carrier monkeys. Their job is to pick up and attract whatever the latest and greatest germ, bug, or virus is and then bring it home to share with the rest of the family. We teach our children to share, but we fail miserably to distinguish between germs and the good stuff. Having three kids in twenty-six months was pretty close to having twins with a spare; therefore, they passed everything back and forth to each other. The best, actually the *worst*, thing we passed around was a particularly nasty piece of work known as the ROTO-Virus.

A few years back they tried to vaccinate against this thing, but then decided the vaccine was worse than actual virus, which blows my mind because, having lived through the virus,

I cannot really imagine anything being worse. You see, I was pregnant (I start a lot of sentences like that because it seems like I was *always* pregnant) with Elliott, and this all went down around Easter of that year. Ethan wasn't feeling well; he'd had some sort of tummy bug and it was coming out the diapered end, but not the top. Emma seemed to be in good shape. Praises on that one. I felt lousy, but that's how I felt while pregnant. If my eyes were open, I was throwing up...I mean "glowing"...

Well, it was Easter weekend, so Jeff and I packed up the kids and headed to Austin because this was before my parents lost their minds and caught the wander-lust bug to hit the open road on their quest to find America. Through the course of the two-and-a-half-hour drive to Austin, Ethan was getting worse, the diapers were getting more and more volatile, and now Emma seemed to be a bit lethargic. I felt really, *really* lousy, but again...didn't think too much of that. Once we got to Austin, all three of us could do nothing but lie around and let my mother, the Granny, take care of us. For an added bonus, it wasn't just me who was throwing up; Ethan and Emma had started throwing up as well. We were two hours from home. Jeff was fine...so far. In situations like this, it is imperative to keep fluids in little bodies: any type of fluid. Doctors will tell you Pedialyte. That stuff tastes terrible. I mixed Sprite with water, and they liked that. When you've got a kid running a fever and throwing up everything but their toenails, you've got to keep fluids in them. Watered-down Coke or Sprite is the best. It worked for us when were kids, it will do the same for your kids. We munched on saltine crackers and prayed that God would just let us die. It was the worst I've ever felt.

By Easter Sunday, we felt a little better—good enough to head to my grandparent's house for lunch. We didn't make it to church—they don't have couches for us to lie on in the sanctuary. We should've driven straight to Houston because by going to Leander (a little town just outside of Austin), we contaminated my entire family: my grandmother, my grandfather, my great grandmother, two aunts, two uncles, two cousins...not to mention both my parents and all three sisters. I wasn't sure if they would ever let us come back to visit after that one. The ROTO-Virus is like the flu on steroids. It lasted for two weeks. Although it did progressively get less and less, it was still horrible to the nth degree. I fed the kids a lot of bananas and yogurt and applesauce during that time. If you can avoid the ROTO—DO! Oh, Jeff eventually got it, too...no one can escape the ROTO.

Something else I was ill-prepared for was the really weird exotic baby diseases like Mad Cow or Hoof and Mouth. (Although, technically I don't think those are the exact names for them.) The kids—well, one kid (who can remember which one?)—came home with something called Hand, Foot, and Mouth Disease, which I promptly forgot the name of, so I switched it to Hoof and Mouth. Then, as I was explaining this to my mother, she thought it was Mad Cow, and so the story goes. HFM (Hand, Foot, and Mouth) starts with a fever, and then after the fever is gone, that's when the rash appears. The rash is inside the mouth like little blisters or ulcers. It really drives the kids nuts. I felt bad for them. The rash can also show up the palms of their hands or the soles of their feet, hence the name "Hand, Foot, and Mouth." Adults don't typically get it. And kids, once they hit ten, outgrow their chances of getting it. We've had it three times in this house. Good times. But don't freak out if it visits you. It doesn't mean you are dirty or in need of a personal hygiene lesson... even though that was my first thought. I'm here to tell you that kids pick up germs everywhere! They are a magnet for them. And it doesn't help that their favorite way to tell what something is, is to put it in their mouth. And all God's sisters said...GROSS!

Once Elliott arrived, that pretty much secured me a front-row parking spot at the pediatrician's office. I was there every week. It brought me closer to my pediatrician, who is now one of my very good friends. Our families have vacationed to Disney World together; we even have timeshare condos with the same company—though at the time of purchase we didn't know it! We thought when Ethan had tubes put in his ears, that would fix most of his major ailments, but as the old saying goes...that's what we get for thinking. I told you we had not seen the last of Dr. Chan, the ENT. Each time the winds of change blew through the great city of Houston, those winds kicked up new pollutants, new pollen spores, and new sources of gunk that sent Ethan's immune system into a literal tailspin.

Bronchitis and pneumonia were two maladies we had become quite familiar with. Imagine my surprise when my doctor suggested that Ethan have his tonsils removed. Upper respiratory infections, sinus infections, and every level of bronchitis we had dealt with...but strep throat was fortunately something we had escaped. I was wracking my brain—I could only think of once, and that was a big maybe, that we'd ever had the pleasure of having strep in the house. I thought multiple cases of strep throat was the major reason why kids had their tonsils removed. Why in the world would our pediatrician suggest removing Ethan's tonsils?

Do you know what the primary function of your tonsils are? Don't worry, I didn't either. Allow me to enlighten you. The primary role of your tonsils is to catch all the garbage that comes into your body through your mouth and nose (basically). They are filters. They are trappers. They catch the garbage and then dispose of it. The problem occurs when the garbage coming in presents too much of a workload for the tonsils. Then, they just catch all the garbage and hold onto it. Once that happens, they grow and grow and grow. The tonsils are located in the back of the throat, on either side; they shouldn't touch. When they get so full of yuckiness, they swell, like a garbage bag. That's where we were with Ethan: His tonsils had stopped doing their job. They were no longer getting rid of the junk; now they were simply hoarding the junk. His tonsils were so enlarged that they were kissing. It was time for them to go.

Having your tonsils and adenoids (just another extension of the tonsils) removed is a fairly routine surgery. At least that's what I would've told anyone whose child was going in for this operation. That's what people told me. I'm here to tell you, statistics don't mean jack when it's your kid going under the knife. A tonsillectomy doesn't take very long to perform. But the waiting is excruciating.

A word of advice to any parent whose child will undergo surgery: Hit the gym everyday for a couple of weeks *before* your child's big day. If your kiddo is like any of mine—they will wake up from anesthesia swinging for the fence. You will need any and all the extra strength you can muster to fight them off! When you watch TV and you see people waking up from surgery, they seem a bit disoriented and groggy, but otherwise fine—y'all, that is staged for TV. If you ever see children doing that, they are made out of plastic!

Jeff and I were sitting in the waiting room blindly flipping through magazines when a nurse came out to get us. We thought it was pretty fast, but that was about all we had time to think about because as soon as we took two steps toward the door she came out of, we heard it. There was a scream that sounded like a caged wild animal, something low and guttural coming from the direction that we were heading. The sound was growing louder. We passed through a set of double doors, and still the sound grew louder. *Somebody's not having a very good day*, I thought quietly to myself. We walked through another door, and still the sound grew more frantic and louder still. The nurses were looking at us intensely now.

My heart started racing as we walked through the last door and headed for a secluded room, passed the rows of children (*real* children) who actually were sitting up in their beds eating popsicles. None of them were screaming. I looked through the window of this little room, and saw a child possessed and two nurses distraught. Ethan was in a full breach, arms spread wide, mouth wide open, trying desperately to escape the death grip these two nurses had on him. His eyes were closed. I doubt his legs would've supported him, had he tried to stand. I threw open the door and grabbed him. He calmed immediately. I sank into a chair. Truth be told, I almost fainted. He was still attached to his IV, he was scared, he was hurting, and he was five years old. The worst part of this: it was only the beginning.

After a tonsillectomy, you can expect your kiddo to be down for three or four days, a week at worst. I'm a firm believer in the fact that kids are manufactured by Rubbermaid. They bounce back with exceptional speed. This was not the case with Ethan. After four days of lying around and not eating much, he still was not up and around. Knowing that my kids leaned a bit toward the dramatic side of life, I honestly thought he was milking the whole "I just had surgery, pity me" thing. I was wrong. Somewhere around a week after his surgery, he began to tell me that one of his legs hurt. Odd, I thought. The kid had his tonsils taken out, and they are a ways away from his leg. Being filled with kindness and compassion and having a four-year-old and a three-year-old running through the house, I told him his leg hurt because he had not used it in a week, and he needed to get up and move around. He was supremely obedient in those days, so he slowly swung his legs over the side of the couch, tried to stand up, and quickly hit the ground. His legs simply would not support him. He began to cry. I became concerned. I picked him up, and put him back on the couch and took a good look at him. His left leg, from the knee down, was swollen, and there were purple dots emerging sporadically all over both legs. I was thinking, *This can't be good.* Turns out, it wasn't good. Before my husband got home from work, both legs had started to swell, along with his elbows and his hands. They were tender to the touch. I was trying to be concerned without showing him how bothered I was by this. Twenty-four hours later, there was no change, so we headed to the ER.

The ER doctor was brilliant. We got in right away. We told her he had just had his tonsils taken out about a week earlier. The dawn of understanding spread wide across her face. Here's the skinny on what happened, in a nutshell: Ethan's tonsils were so full of nastiness, that the first cut to take them out flooded his little body with toxins. His immune system bailed on him. His body was literally shutting down against this onslaught of poison coursing through it. Bottom line: There was nothing we do. The purple spots were from his blood vessels, which were leaking. The blood in his stool was because the blood vessels in his kidneys were leaking, along with the lining of his stomach. There is no medicine for this. You wait it out. You pray. It's called Henoch-Schonlein Purpura. I've never been so afraid in my life. Over the next six weeks (because that's how long it took for this horrible thing to "run its course"), I did some major bartering with God: begging, pleading, whatever you want to call it. There was nothing but God's grace and mercy to keep these toxins from attacking the blood vessels in Ethan's heart or his brain. If the toxins went for his heart or his brain, we would lose him. We needed a miracle. This "reaction" happens to one in about five hundred thousand kids. But, as I said earlier, statistics don't mean jack when it's your kid.

Spending six weeks home with Ethan had taken its toll on me. I followed him around constantly. I was so afraid he would need something. Or that he would fall down. He was a little bitty thing before his surgery, and then after it—my word! He lost almost ten pounds! I could pick him up and carry him around in one arm. He didn't have all his strength. He drank a lot of those Boost drinks for kids; I mixed them with ice cream and made little shakes for him. He was my easy kid. I'm thankful. It made it easier for me one afternoon, when I got the phone call from school...

Me: Hello?

Office: Dallas, we need you to come and get Elliott.

Me: Why? Is he okay?

Office: Yeah, he's okay...but, he shoved a playground rock up his nose. I can't reach it. He's freaking out. We need you to come and get him.

Me: Terrific. I'm on my way.

In every house, there's *one*. Elliott is my *one*. Although, in light of the last story, you'd think it'd be Ethan. Nope. It's Elliott. The thing about playground rocks is this: They are little, so they fit up a nose. They are pretty, so they are tempting to put in your pockets. They also fit into ears, although with ears they usually pop right out. Noses are a different story completely. Two reasons: (1) you can push up with your finger, while (2) you suck in with your breath. Both of these actions, when combined, create the problem. So, I had to go get Elliott, while calling Dr. Chan's offices trying to get an emergency appointment to remove a playground rock.

It's a good thing I don't mind being the center of attention because as I was hanging up with the nurse at his office, I could hear them laughing. Unfortunately, we did not make it to the office before the rock made the turn from the bridge of the nose into No Man's Land. I guess the urge to sniff was too great. Another good thing about playground rocks is their size. What goes up and in, must come down and out. I'll let you ponder that for a moment about the path the rock may have taken as it exited the body... (For those who may not be as well acquainted with the anatomy of nasal passages as I have had to be, allow me to elaborate slightly. Most of the time, things you are able to suck *up* through your nose, you are also able to swallow *down* your throat and *into* your tummy...where it will eventually follow the same pathway as food in order to leave the body. This same principle is applied to playground rocks simply because of their size. Can I get a collective "gross"? That concludes today's anatomy lesson.)

It was little more than a year after Ethan's surgery and subsequent L-O-N-G recovery that I found myself sitting in my pediatrician's office with Elliott, listening to her hand me yet another pneumonia diagnosis for him. She recommended Elliott have his tonsils removed as well. You can just imagine how fired up I was to jump on that opportunity. She had to do some pretty smooth talking and super convincing to assure me that Elliott's surgery would go much better. Elliott was a year younger than Ethan at the time of his surgery; however he would also be having his sinuses scraped. Ick. Thankfully, Elliott was the poster child for the recovery...except for the *initial* recovery. He, too, came out fighting like a tiger. I was beginning to think they saved this isolation room just for us.

In the days following his operation, I watched him like a hawk. I was sure that purple dots would emerge and that his appendages would swell. No such luck. He was back to his usual self within the prescribed timeframe. I thought we were out of the woods. Think again. I had to fight to keep Elliott at home and on the couch. He felt good, so he wanted to play; he didn't understand why he could not run and play. When I finally felt comfortable enough to send him to school, he was all smiles and raring to go. His surgery was just a tad bit dif-

ferent than his brother's. They both had their tonsils and adenoids taken out, but Elliott's surgery was a bit more involved
in the fact that his sinuses were scraped. It made his operation last longer. He came into recovery looking like Hannibal
Lector. His nose was packed with gauze and he had a drip
pad taped under his nose. Ugh! I'm getting queasy just thinking about it! Doing a sinus scrape on a set of little sinuses is
tedious and slow-going.

A few weeks after he'd had a chance to heal, naturally
the doc wanted to take a look. Think about this for a minute:
Where are your sinuses? Under your eyes and *up your nose,*
right? How do you suppose the doc is going to get a peek up
there? Doctors have fabulous little tools and toys. Dr. Chan is
no exception. He had this long and skinny scope that he was
going to use to look up Elliott's nose just to check and make
sure the stitches were dissolving and everything was moving
right along.

Let's just pause right there for a minute.

If you've never taken your child to a doctor who does not
have children, I highly recommend that you try one out at
least once. They are so much fun to mess with! Y'all, I'm not a
doctor. At the time of Elliott's follow-up appointment, I had
no idea what this man was about to attempt with my son. If
I had caught on a little sooner, I would have suggested something or someone a little more sturdy than myself to use as
the *only* means of restraint.

So, I was sitting in this chair with Elliott on my lap, and
Dr. Chan said, "Okay, Mom. I'm going to need you to give
him a good hug while I look up his nose." It was laughable. He
started coming at Elliott with this skinny little scope that was

about the width and length of a pipe cleaner, while I was trying desperately to get him into a pretzel hold—which wasn't working. He tried to pry Elliott's head back, so he could put the scope up his nose; meanwhile, Elliott got one hand lose—grabbed the scope, and made his own pretzel. All movement from all parties involved stopped immediately. Dr. Chan just looked at me, stood up, and excused himself from the exam room.

There's something you need to know about our ENT. Yes, he's Asian, as evident by his name. He's one of the best in Houston. He's one of the most mild-mannered men I've ever met. He stands somewhere around six feet tall. He wears ostrich skin cowboy boots with his scrubs. His IQ hovers just above brilliant, yet he relates to people well, even children.

When Elliott snapped his scope, I swear smoke came out of this man's ears. It took fifteen minutes for him to come back in the room with us. He managed a quick look in Elliott's throat and in his ears—but wisely left his nose alone. Then, the nurse came in to check us out. I apologized profusely. She smiled sweetly, and said, "Wow. Didn't know that scope could bend like that. You'd think for four thousand dollars, it'd be a little bit stronger."

I told you, Elliott's is my *one*. Four grand...gone in four seconds.

Awesome.

· · · · · ·

Having doctors as friends comes in handy, especially when you've got a kid like Elliott. By the age of seven, he'd had three concussions and broken his nose at least once—the jury is still out on the second time. Granted, they've all been mild, but a head injury is a head injury. The kid has no fear! I have enough fear, after watching him bust himself silly, for the both of us. He's had three CAT scans and I've lost count on the chest x-rays...but if he undergoes anymore radiation we can use him for a power source the next time a hurricane blows through Houston.

One of the times he decided to tear himself up was, thankfully, in front of my pediatrician. We figured out, after having three kids each, that our kids are almost the exact same age. I never claimed to be incredibly bright. Our kids are lined up in the exact order: boy, girl, boy, although hers are spaced out just a wee bit further apart than mine are.

So, one summer they were over swimming, when Elliott came tearing around the corner. He turned to look over his shoulder, tripped over his own feet, and bit it—big time. He smacked his head—face first—into the bottom step of the hot tub. Blood, big knot, tears...we had everything...not to mention five other kids rushing to see what just happened. Naturally, the force of the blow cracked the cartilage across his nose, thus causing it to break.

The flagstone step is a tad bit harder than his forehead, which resulted in a mild concussion. All I can say is that I'm glad I had a witness! Elliott is forever doing stuff like that! Each and every time he does that, I get to spend two nights on the floor beside his bed, waking him up every two hours:

"Ellie, what's your name?"

"Elliott."

"What's my name?"

"Mommy."
"What's my other name?"
"Dallas."

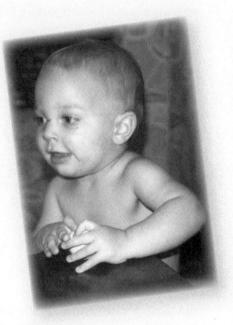

Look closely, and you can
see the line across his nose
and the shadow under both
eyes! This was the first
broken nose...

I don't have an awful lot to contribute from Emma in this
chapter. She doesn't try to skydive off the roof; she doesn't
really jump curbs on her bike. She does, however, go mattress-
surfing down the stairs, thanks to the *Princess Diaries* movies.
But I can live with that. She would like to break something,
though; preferably her leg. She wants crutches. I think that's
why she mattress-surfs. Boys are just different. Boys are very
active. They just *go*. They just *do*. They just *are*.

My children have the privilege to go to a private school. For
my husband and I, it means they get individual attention and
an education based on the beliefs and foundation of the Bible.
For our children, it means they cannot ride a big yellow school

bus, so they are always car-riders. One day, I was walking out the door of my house getting ready to go pick them up from school, when the phone rang. It was the school. I thought, *This cannot be good.* The day was almost over. Whatever it was had to be bad enough that it couldn't wait the fifteen minutes until the final bell.

Me: Hello?

Office: Hi Dallas, this is the nurse.

Me: Hey. Who do you have?

Office: I have Ethan. I don't want to worry you, but he took a pretty good blow to the head—

Me: He *what*?!

Office: Well, he was on the pavilion at recess, playing kick-ball, and he was sliding into home; he misjudged his distance and hit the fence. He's okay. But he is bleeding pretty good.

Me: Does he need stitches?

Office: I don't think so...but we did have to change his shirt.

Me: Keep him with you, I'm on my way. I'm sending Jeff to get the other two. He's going to the doctor.

Head injuries. They bleed and bleed and bleed. Ethan whacked his head and popped it open in the middle of an eyebrow. I called the pediatrician's office and told them I was on my way. I didn't ask them if they had time. I told them the situation, and said we were on our way. Our doctor is always pretty handy with a needle and surgical thread. The other thing with head wounds is that if you ice them, they don't bleed as much, but as soon as you take the ice off—BAM! You are back to full flow. I don't really do very well with blood. It isn't really my gift.

Ethan was so excited! I can't even tell you!

See, it's boy thing. He was excited about not crying on the playground. He was playing kickball with the older kids, and he was sliding into home. Well he over-shot it a bit and hit the wrought iron post behind him. He didn't cry. He did tell me his stomach hurt a little when he saw all the blood, but he was very brave. Mom was brave, too...until we got to the doctor's office.

They put us into a room right away. On the drive out to the office, Ethan didn't have an icepack on his head, so it had opened back up. Once we got inside the office, and I could see it—Mom was getting quite a bit queasy. So, the nurses fixed him up with a new icepack and took us to a room. He sat in a chair and flipped one-handed through a book (one hand was holding the new icepack on his head), while I lay on the exam table trying to remember my Lamaze breathing in a vain attempt to remain calm. I thought he might be more traumatized if his mother passed out than from the actual injury itself. Plus, I really didn't want Dr. Hanson to have to sew us both up.

When she walked into the room, she laughed out loud at the sight of me on the table, and Ethan sitting in the chair, holding ice on his head. She tried to compose herself, "Uh, Mom? You're going to have to get off the table. I'm going to need it for the patient." I assured her that I knew this, but what she failed to understand was that if I wasn't on this table, she'd quickly have *two* patients. As excited as Ethan was in the beginning about his stitches, when the rubber actually started to hit the road, his mind began to change. He decided maybe stitches wasn't the way to go. Lucky for him, she agreed. He needed glue. Superglue. *Surgical* superglue. Faster than stitches, burns like FIRE. But, the upside: He did get to go to school with white tape over his eyebrow, and everyone knows that the chicks dig battle wounds.

There have been so many times over the past nine years when I just didn't think I could get through another night. Some of the days were rough, too. But the nights seemed to be the hardest, especially when the kids were sick. I never realized until I was watching that *Raymond* episode that I, too, can tell when my kids have a fever by the touch. I know when they are faking it. I know when something is wrong. I have built a network of mommy friends to help me, a network to bounce ideas off of and to pull even better ideas from. If you're reading this book and you've got a little one that is two years old or younger, be prepared: that kid will be sick until he turns three. Then it's like magic; their immune system kicks in, and the ailments level off. But, then he's three and he's the devil dressed like an angel...but that's another chapter. Diaper rash cream isn't only for bottoms. During cold and flu season, when little noses are just raw from being wiped and wiped all the time, put some diaper rash cream on them at night before bed—just please use a clean tube—and don't get them confused. Triple-antibiotic ointment plus diaper rash cream on a very persistent diaper rash will help immensely. Throw some regular corn starch on there as well, and baby's bottom will feel much better in no time. Those are just little tidbits I learned along the way. I wish someone had told me with my first one, instead of figuring that out on my own with my third.

I spent weeks on the floor in various kids' rooms. I'm not sure what I thought that would accomplish. I think it was for my benefit rather than theirs. A stuffy baby is a miserable mommy. And a child that doesn't feel well will act out in brutal ways against you and their siblings. While you know they are sick, the rules of the house do not change. It confuses them when the rules change.

I have a friend who has four children. We've already established the fact that we need to set boundaries in place around our children in order to protect them and to keep them safe. Well, my friends have a rule about sitting on the coffee table. The rule is "don't." We have the same rule at our house. Their youngest son, let's call him Evan (I like "E" names), had been home from school for a couple of days. He was suffering from the coughing and stuffy gunk that had been going around down here. His older sister, we'll call her Emily, noticed that her little brother was sitting on top of the coffee table, and this was a huge no-no in their house.

She proceeded to try and remove her little brother from the coffee table. In her defense, she did first try to persuade him verbally to get off the table, to which he replied, "You're not the boss of me." I can assure you this was not the welcomed response that eight-year-old Emily was looking for. She diplomatically tried again. Nothing. In fact, Evan scooted himself back a little further toward the middle of the coffee table. This small but mighty move of sheer defiance enraged his older sister so much that she was really past the point of reason. So, she got up from her place on the couch, walked over to her six-year-old brother, and began to yank on his legs. Evan kicked and fought and screamed, but Emily had two years and quite a bit more bulk to her frame than he did. Down off the coffee table came Evan—*straight* down in fact. Onto the floor, without time to brace himself or reposition, he landed on his right elbow.

Can't you just hear it crunch? I did. A little bit of background info: Evan had broken that same elbow six months earlier when he fell off the monkey bars at school. What was Emily's response to their mother over the wailing sobs of her brother? "Mother, I had to get him off the coffee table. If he had stayed up there, he might have gotten hurt!"

Kids do funny things. They say funny things. They shove things up their noses and in their ears. They break equipment that costs four thousand dollars. (That one still stings, but then again, that's why doctors have really good insurance. And I bet after Elliott's little mishap, the doctor papooses kids down now, instead of relying on the sole talents, strengths, and abilities of Mom, the Wonder Woman, to hold them down.) My kids move fast most days, but when they are sick, they snuggle and cuddle. I worry over them and I fuss over them. I pray they don't get sick. I would not go back to the under-two timeframe for all the tea in China or gold in the world. And now, when I see Elliott standing at the top of the jungle gym at school, my heart still sinks, I still cringe, I still wonder how many stitches will it take to sew him up, but I smile as I grab my notebook and think, *What are they going to do next?*

Addendum

How's this for Murphy's Law? During the first edit of this book, my two boys decided to give me material that was just too good to pass up! In April of each year, my church has an annual family camping trip to a local state park. Sign-up sheets get passed around, families converse back and forth about who is going, who wants to be placed next to whom, and so on and so forth. Naturally, we signed up to go. Remember Nelson? Upon arriving at the park, our kids were instantly drawn to this big ditch across the way from the campsites that played host to numerous fallen pine trees, hollow logs, rocks...in short, this was a kid's dream come true. Also laying across this ditch was an old two by four board that happened to be the perfect size for a swing. My husband, being the masterful engineer that he is, found a long rope and somehow managed to fashion a swing of sorts using this piece of wood and one of the fallen trees. The kids (almost forty of them!) absolutely loved this setup! It seemed to be the ideal playground equipment. About a day and a half into our three-day trip, we hear screams of panic and pain coming from the ditch moving closer and closer to camp. Naturally, the adults in the vicinity sprang into action. The bigger kids were among the first to make it to us.

"Ethan is hurt! He's hurt real bad!" My heart actually stopped. There were about fifteen kids in all that had been congregated at the ditch, and three of them had made it to us before we saw Ethan walking toward the campground. I must say, I was relieved to see that he was still upright. He was indeed crying, but from the front, he looked okay. It wasn't until I got closer to him that I realized "okay" was not the proper word. He was screaming, "My head! My head is open! I'm going to die!" As I looked at the back of his head, I noticed a silver-dollar-sized hole had been knocked in the back of him. My knees buckled. I instinctively reached for the open wound with my hand to try apply pressure in order to stop the copious amount of blood that was just free-flowing from my son's head. It was an absolute miracle that he was still on his feet. In between murmured words of comfort to him, I was shouting scathing words of fire at the other children, demanding that someone tell me how this happened.

My line of fire landed on the poor child that was the accident source. Bless his heart. Apparently, William was swinging (as all the kids had done over the last couple of days) when Ethan bent down to pick up a stick. As Ethan stood up, William and the swing collided with the back of Ethan's head, thus popping the skin clean open, exposing the bone. I've never been so scared in my life. William was almost as hysterical as Ethan. He honestly thought Ethan was going to die, and that if he did, it would be all his fault. And, at that moment in time, I did nothing to dissuade his way of thinking. That was one of my lowest moments in parenting. This was an accident—a *bloody and gruesome* accident, but still, an accident.

Do you have a sixth sense? I think I do. But only sometimes. Earlier that morning, as we were all sitting around drinking our coffee, during a lull in the conversation, I happened to ask the circle at large if anyone knew where the closest emergency room was. They all just looked at me as though I had just sprouted pretty pink polka dots. At the time, it was a very random question. I explained to them that, here we were, in the middle of nowhere, with close to forty kids... I figured *someone* was going to make a trip to the ER. I had no idea that in less than three hour's time, it would be *us*.

One of our friends, Lesli, grabbed a towel as my hand was

doing an exceptionally poor job of stopping the blood flow, and hopped into the back seat of Jeff's truck ready to make the thirty-mile, one-way trip to the Livingston Memorial Hospital. I'm pretty sure Jeff broke some earlier land speed records to get us there. It amazes me how well we react to a crisis. During the ride to the hospital, I was calm, I was collected, and I did what I needed to do. I kept the pressure on Ethan's head. I talked to him, made sure he knew who he was, who I was, etc. However, once we got to the hospital, all of my capabilities must have stayed in the truck. Signing him in at the registration desk, I could feel my knees getting weaker and weaker. Walking back to the triage room, I was getting hotter and hotter, and you know how cold hospitals are. Ten minutes after our arrival at the hospital, we were settled into an exam room. The nurse came in through the door, greeted Ethan, looked at me, opened her mouth to speak, but Ethan beat her to it. He said, "Uh, Mom...you don't look so good." He was right. The nurse agreed. Jeff moved pretty fast, too. The nurse, chimed in, "Yeah Mom, we're gonna need you to get on the floor as fast as you can." Too late.

My knees buckled, and I was down! Jeff was there to make sure our sweet nurse didn't have two head wounds to sew up. That's about the time Lesli came walking back into the room. She'd stepped out to make a quick phone call back to camp. The sight that greeted her was almost comical. Ethan was sitting on the exam table, I was on the floor with the nurse, and Jeff was huddled over me. Evidently, my adrenaline stopped once I turned Ethan over to the hospital staff. I was fine, just a little too woozy to be on my feet; we all thought it best if I stayed on the floor.

Ethan was such a trouper! He got four staples in the back of his head and a swell, V-shaped scar. He's totally pumped about the scar. I think it's a boy thing. Jeff is very proud of all of *his* scars, too. We left the hospital with an icepack for Ethan's head, an icepack for me (should I get lightheaded again), and memories for a lifetime! Two and a half weeks later, the staples came out. However the scar is still there... right smack-dab in the middle of the back of his head.

Ethan could have doubled as a Civil War soldier after the bandage the hospital put on him!

Boys!

Now, not to be outdone by his big brother, Elliott has a little something else to contribute to this chapter as well. I told you, he is my *one*. Every family has one. Elliott seems to be ours. This child is not afraid of anything! He will try anything. He will jump, dive, climb off or over any structure or cliff or rock you put in his path. In the long run, I think this will serve him well...provided he lives through childhood. Two weeks before the school year ended, I received yet another phone call from the school nurse. Caller ID is a wonderful thing. Anytime the school's name and number pops up in my window, I do a mental rundown as to who our nurse could possibly have in her office. I must say that I was ill-prepared for the conversation that took place on that day.

I happened to be on campus when she called. I picked up my phone only to be greeted with, "Hey Dallas, we think Elliott broke his arm. We need you to come and get him." *He did what?!* I'm sorry; did I say earlier in the book that we'd not had to deal with broken bones? I was wrong. Here we are, within eight short weeks of each other, dealing with wide-open, blood-gushing head wounds, and now a broken arm. The next book I write will be an exposé on the top ten hospitals of East Texas!

Needless to say, I ran to the nurse's office and found Elliott being cradled by the school secretary, arm iced and splinted, crocodile tears in his eyes, and waiting for me to come and get him. Poor little guy. I was curious about how this all went down. He and his friends were playing a game. He was evading capture from the enemies, who incidentally were throwing fireballs at him, and he did his best *Mission Impossible* vault over the side of the *highest slide* on the playground landing in perfect push-up position, thus resulting in the CRACK of his right radius. Awesome. Now we get to visit yet another emergency room. Twenty-four hours later, Elliott was the proud owner of a royal-blue, waterproof cast. I'm leery to say we are done with ER visits; after all, I still have one more child. Honestly, I'm surprised she really has not thrown herself down the stairs! She wants crutches so she can duct tape them in pretty, fashionable colors, and figures she needs to break a leg to get them. I'm almost certain she is devising a plan to obtain them. Lucky for her, I've just special-ordered a large quantity of bubble-wrap from eBay. When it arrives, I'm wrapping her in it to keep her extra safe!

Kids! What are you gonna do?

Elliott was so proud of his cast! There's a lot less fuss to a cast than staples! Is it any wonder why I held up better this time around?

November, 2006, We were trying for: hear no evil, see no evil, speak no evil... It didn't exactly work out!

The Bark Park

· · · · · · · · · · · · · · · · · ·

When I went to California, I was at the mercy of my sisters. I had no vehicle of my own, so I went where they went. One of my sisters wanted to take her dog to the dog park located in Balboa Park. I've never been to a dog park before. I thought it might be fun, and besides, what were my other options? Flower, a little Boston Terrier, was super excited to be going for a ride in the car! She loves to ride. She's not much different than a child. I had no idea just how closely related to children dogs were until we arrived at the Bark Park.

The idea behind a place like the Bark Park is to have a confined area in the city where your dog can run around unleashed and be free. They can play with other dogs and bark and just have a good time. I was amazed at all the different types of dogs inside the park. There were little bitty Chihuahuas, mid-sized mutts, and even some very large, strap-a-saddle-on-them Great Danes. Everyone was playing, and everyone was getting along. The owners were standing in little groups watching their "kids" play. You could hear the conversations between the dogs as they'd go racing by:

Flower: Chase me!

Other dog: No, you chase me!

Next dog: Run this way!

Flower: Okay!

Then, off they'd zoom...back and forth...back and forth. I found myself getting as nervous for Flower as I would my own kids, had we been at a people park. But Flower, like my kids, was making her own way. She was having fun. She was on an even and level playing field. All the dogs were on level ground...until someone pulled out...the *toy*.

One toy can ruin a good and harmonious day. With the arrival of that one toy, there was a literal shift in the Earth's rotation. Groups of dogs who had been running and playing in perfect peace had now turned on each other, showing teeth and growling and using their "angry voices." Flower immediately started to chase a different dog, and then proceeded to jump on the dog's owner when he bent down to pick up his own dog. My poor sister had to run all the way across the park in order to catch Flower who already had a considerable head start. Flower did not want to listen to my sister. She did not want to leave the park. In fact, it was a bizarre battle of wills to see who would actually win this odd power struggle. Everything went upside down over the arrival of a Frisbee.

This was exactly like children. Odd power struggles occur every day. Our kids are going to test their boundaries each and every day. We know that no matter where the limits are set on them, they will push and push until they get one toe over the line, and then stand there to see just what exactly we are going to do about it. The only comfort in this scenario is that they do this with their friends, too. So, it isn't just us that they are testing.

When all of my kids were little and in preschool, very seldom did a day pass that a note did not get sent home informing me that one of them bit someone else. At the preschool that my kids attended when they were little, the teachers would write these very sweet "Happy Notes" to be sent home at the end of the day. I looked forward to those notes. I cherished these notes. The "Happy Notes" were not as frequent a visitor in our house as their opposite counterpart. Because, as I mentioned, I had three kids in the same preschool, therefore, it was a given that something would go wrong every single day. What you did not want to see in your child's cubby was a red note. This was a "Sad Face Note" informing you that Junior had enough difficulties that day to warrant a red note; in short, not one redeeming quality could be found in your child to give him a Happy Note for the day. Considering the fact that I had three kids at one time in the same preschool, you could bet dollars to doughnuts that at least one of them every Tuesday or Thursday was going to have a red note in their cubby. It was a super-double-terrific day when there was more than one red note on the same day.

Cry.

But, why? What would they do? What could be so bad that they could get these pint-sized disciplinary action forms? I mentioned in passing several chapters ago that we referred to Elliott as our little piranha. That's true. He was. What I failed to divulge is that the other two fit that category as well. All three of them are champion biters. They come by it honestly. My mother was notorious for her biting. I'm pretty sure she bit her friends 'til she was ten or eleven. Stories about my mother and her biting are legendary in parts of the Texas Hill Country. So, I'm going with genetics on this one.

My theory behind the biting is two-fold: one, it's the age-old, bottom-line, good, old-fashioned power struggle. Someone has a toy that someone else wants. When they don't get their way—they bare their teeth...literally. The second part of this theory sort of goes hand-in-hand with the first—when you are as little as my kids are (and I do mean little, as in size), and a bigger kid starts pushing you around, your chompers become the most effective means of self-defense. Now, the threat can be real or perceived. Either way, the teeth are gonna be shown, and someone is probably going to bleed.

I just knew that my kids were going to be the first kids ever kicked out of this Christian preschool for cannibalism. I simply could not get a handle on the biting thing. The kicker was—they only did it at school...in the beginning. Each one of my children had received so many red notes that I could've re-papered the downstairs bathroom. That's a lot of teeth marks on their friends. Up to that point, not one of them ever tried to sink their teeth into me. However, eventually, even good criminals slip up. Each one of my kids bit me *one time*. Only once. You see, at school, the administration is bound by certain limitations. There are only certain means to which they can carry out their disciplines. All of my little savages were read to: sweet little books about how we bite apples and not our friends. Give me a break. When you've got a two-year-old purposefully going for blood, reading her a book about biting apples is not going to get the message across. They also sat in time-out at school. That was probably a safe bet at the time, but in all actuality, it just gave them time to plot out their next attack.

You see, with me, I am a visual learner. I learn best when I can see what it is I'm supposed to be learning. You can tell me what you want me to learn, but if you *show* me *while* you tell me, I've a much better chance of retaining that information. Our children operate on the same level. Every time I would get to school and see one of those stinking red notes sticking out of a cubby, I would first engage the filter over my mouth so as not to spit fire at my sweet innocents, and then try and wrack my brain to figure out how to tell my kids in a way that they would understand that biting your friends will make you not have any friends. But again, when talking to a two- or a three-year-old, reason just doesn't play a very big role. I needed a way to *show* them. As it turns out, I just needed to be patient. One by one, the kids forgot who they were dealing with. They forgot that I am their mother and not one of their little friends from school, so when they came at me with an open mouth, fangs bared...I bit them back.

Again, I have to stress to you, *I did not hurt my children*. I would never hurt them. I did, however, get their attention. I had my moment. And now, I had the opportunity to tell them that biting is hurtful *and* I had the opportunity to show them how it hurts. While they left full upper and lower teeth marks in me, I left no such marks on them, but the act of biting them registered greatly on the "hurt feelings" scale. Up until that point, while they had been told several times that biting hurts, they didn't actually connect the dots until after *they* got bit. You cannot reason with a one-, two-, three-, or even a four-year-old. They need boundaries and limits. Parenting is all about timing. You have to be patient and be able to outlast your children. They have the advantage in this department, I'm afraid to say, so we, as parents, must be vigilant.

There are reasons why we do the things we do as parents. I could not allow my children to continue biting other people's children. I had to find a solution to that problem. Well, I did. It required me to wait and be patient, and to give them a taste of their own medicine. Kids are so very smart; they know when you're bluffing. They know when you are running on low battery life and the threats you are giving don't really hold water.

Take, for instance, staying in their car seats. For some reason, remaining buckled securely in their seatbelts goes against every fiber of their being. They do not understand that we have not invented car seats as a new way to deliver endless hours of torture and punishment to them. They do not understand that if they do not remain securely fastened into these seats, that Mom gets the ticket from the local law, and could run the risk of losing this strong-willed child to the authorities. All they know is that this five-point harness system is the devil, and it is imposing an immediate threat to their well-being and mental health, and therefore, they must fight, fight, fight to the death with everything inside their tiny bodies to rid themselves of these horrible and evil contraptions.

With the way my oldest child screamed each time we put him in his car seat, you would have thought we had installed hot pokers or sharp nails up the back side of his seat. I thought children *liked* riding in cars. That's the way they look on TV. All the children in the movies seem to calm right down when Mom or Dad put them in the car...in fact, that was the one way their parents could calm them down when all else had failed.

Not my son!

No, he screamed until I thought he would choke. I inevitably would have to pull over halfway to the grocery store (which was a whopping ten minutes from my house), climb into the back seat, and check to make sure that I had not done something terribly wrong to his seat. To my relief and dismay (from all the racket he was making, you'd think—or at least hope—there would be a reason), the straps were fine; he was simply mad. This went on and on and on until he was old enough to face forward. Turns out, Ethan isn't the only one who doesn't like riding in cars. Well, check that, cars are okay; it's the seatbelts, car seats, and any other type of restraining system you can think of that make the trip unbearable.

I have a sweet friend of mine who is going through something similar with her daughter to what I went through with Ethan. The difference is that her daughter is four years old. This kid is super smart and knows exactly where Mom's buttons are and exactly how to push them. If you've never watched a child in action before, I highly recommend it. A word to the wise: make sure it is someone *else's* child...when it's *your* child, the lesson isn't nearly as entertaining. As this pair was leaving my house one night, goodbyes were especially hard, and her daughter was having an extremely difficult time getting out the front door. I offered to "help." I carried her stuff (the bag, shoes, miscellaneous clothing) to the car, while she struggled to get a good grip on her wiggling, screaming, and fighting child.

"I DON'T WANT TO GO HOME! I WANT TO STAY FOR DINNER! I JUST WANNA EAT DINNER HERE! DON'T TAKE ME!"

My friend, Amanda (not really her name), managed to get this pint-size prize-fighter into the back seat and seated in her car seat, but had yet to get her buckled. As this peanut was still four years old and didn't weigh very much, a five-point harness system was required for her safety. Amanda had succeeded in fastening one side of the leg straps, when all of a sudden, in a move of sheer genius on her daughter's part, she screams, "You're hurting me!"

Now, if I had not been watching the whole thing, I would

not have believed this. Amanda's hands flew into the air, she raised up and backed away so fast from her child that she hit her head on the top of her car, and the best part of the whole thing was the smug and satisfied look on this four-year-old's face. She had just struck pure, baby-guilt gold. Amanda turned around and looked at me. She slowly stood to her full upright position, leaving her fully enraged daughter to still sit and scream in the car, and with her own tears in her eyes asked, "What do I do?"

Girls, I'm here to tell you, buckle them in! Amanda was in no way, shape, or form hurting her daughter. She was doing the right thing by obeying the law and keeping her child safe by keeping her in her car seat. Had her child been allowed to roam through the car freely, she would have endangered her life as well as her mother's by climbing from the back seat to the front seat and back again with Amanda trying to referee. I put my hands on Amanda's shoulders and looked her square in the eye and told her to finish what she started. Buckle her back in. Use your big-girl voice (not your yelling voice, there is a difference) and remind her that you are the parent, and you will win this round.

I've said before that certain battles are not necessarily hills to die on (remember the hair conditioner all across the bathtub?), but this particular one is. Your child's safety is a life-or-death issue. Buckle them in. I climbed into the driver's seat to watch how this was all going to end, and I was pleased to see that Amanda did get her daughter securely buckled. However, Little Miss Thing was still screaming her sweet little head clean off, and Amanda was suffering greatly from mommy guilt, so she came at her little one with a peace offering in the form of an iPod touch. This was quickly batted away in anger. Amanda reached for it again, to try one more time, but this time, I reached for it. You cannot reward abominable behavior with something fun. Stand your ground. Be the parent. *So what* if they cry all the way home? Let them. How do you deal with noise on that level every time you get into the vehicle? Excedrin, Starbucks, and a loud radio. It will only take two or three times of you outlasting them on issues like this before they realize who is actually in control.

* * * * * *

Meal times are also a fun household battleground. We've gone many rounds over "What's for dinner?" in our kitchen. The most popular answer from me to that question is, "Whatever I put in front of you."

Notice which child is trying to climb out of her chair to avoid eating! Nana could almost always get Emma to eat when I would've just sent her to bed.

Strained peas are just about the most disgusting and unappealing food you can purchase in the grocery store. They look funny and they smell worse. They are, however, essential for your baby's proper growth. In fact, if you stand in the baby food aisle of your local supermarket and take a good long look at all of your jarred choices, you will find just about every vegetable and fruit or combination of the two known to man. Why? Because it is very important that our children have a balanced diet and start off with the proper foundation. Peas are probably my least favorite thing to eat in the whole wide world—and I'll try just about anything. I hated them when I was a kid, and now that I'm a full-grown adult—I still don't like them. I have incredibly vivid memories of my mother serving peas with dinner, and me shoveling spoonfuls of them into my mouth and swallowing them whole with my milk in order to keep myself from having to chew them or taste them. With that said, peas are now a staple in my home. I still don't like them. But I fix them for my children. I fed them to my children when they were babies and in the highchair. I wanted them to be healthy when they were babies. I want them to be healthy now. (Plus, as you remember, frozen peas make excellent icepacks.)

I have two pretty decent eaters, and one challenge. I'll give you three guesses as to which kiddos are my eaters, and which one isn't! My favorite sayings before I had children was "I'll never do..." fill in the blank. "I'll never supplement a bottle for the breast." "I'll never use the TV as a sitter." "I'll never feed my child a cereal bottle." "My child will never act like that."

All I can say now is, "Never say never." It will bite you in the hind-end each and every time. Emma was a particularly difficult baby to feed. She quit nursing very early, most likely because I was already pregnant with her brother (extra helping of mommy guilt on that one), therefore, the bottle was her very best friend. Sleep deprivation makes you entertain all sorts of ideas...like putting rice cereal into your six-week-old's bottle. My mother-in-law first tried to spoon feed it to her...no dice. So then we thought putting cereal in her night-time bottle might be more effective. It was liquid gold. She was in hog heaven...literally. She sucked it right down—every... last...drop. Then she slept for six hours—straight. Of course, that first night, I was up every thirty minutes checking on her, making sure she was still breathing! As she got older, it became more and more of a challenge to find things to put in front of my up-and-coming food critic.

Once Emma learned how to talk, her most favorite thing to say was, "Is this old?" I have no idea where she picked this up from! I would hand her a sippy cup of milk, fresh from the fridge, and she would take it and look from me to the cup and back to me again, and with the voice of an angel ask, "Momma, is this old?" It blew my mind. Plates of food, freshly spooned out of the pans on the stove would get the same quizzical looks, followed by the same question. This went on for two and a half *years*. Of course, now, she doesn't remember that phase, but at the time people thought we had expiration date issues at my house.

The big issue with Emma now is the whole meat thing. Every meat I serve in my house is chicken. It doesn't really matter if it really *is* chicken or not. In her mind, and for the sanity of the other members of the family, we eat chicken every night. Let me explain. Emma really likes chicken. She thinks she doesn't like other meats. She is, of course, completely and utterly mistaken. She eats roast, steak, pork, and even various sausages, but when she was much younger, we (or she, I can't remember who exactly started this) got in the habit of telling her to eat her chicken. It stuck. She is now eight (almost nine) years old and thinks the only thing I know how to cook is chicken. And for some of my friends, this wouldn't be such a bad thing...only serving chicken, that is.

I know plenty of moms out there who behave each and every night as though they were short-order cooks. You know the types—the ones who make a kid-friendly meal consisting of chicken nuggets or hotdogs with mac and cheese on the side. Then they make a completely different and grown-up meal for them and their spouse. (This one is braised veal, couscous, and sautéed green beans.) For those of you that operate your homes this way, can I ask you why you go through the trouble to make two separate meals? Isn't it exhausting?

Now, I get the fact that chicken nuggets with a helping of mac and cheese isn't exactly what most adults would like to have for dinner. I mean, *I* wouldn't eat it for dinner. Do you know that the kids will eat what you put in front of them? I promise, they will. Maybe not at first, but Junior will get hungry enough to eat what is put on his plate.

My dad is a chef; well, he used to be, before he started with the whole big-rig trucking thing. In my opinion, he's one of the best chefs in the country. So, I grew up eating some fairly bizarre things. Why? Daddy wanted to expand my palate. He wanted to expose me and my sisters to all sorts of various foods and flavors. For instance, while most folks across the country celebrated Thanksgiving dinner with a traditional cornbread dressing, we had an oyster based dressing. One of Daddy's favorite kitchen pantry staples was packages of dried seaweed so that we could wrap our own sushi rolls. Another favorite dish that frequented our refrigerator was a Korean fermented vegetable recipe known as kimchi. He wanted us to eat our veggies so we could grow up to be big and strong.

He also wanted to be able to take his four children anywhere and feed us from the menu...or (this one is *super* important) take us to anyone's house without embarrassment. If all we'd been exposed to were chicken nuggets, hotdogs, and macaroni and cheese...what in the world would we eat when invited to Mark and Stephanie's house for dinner, who, incidentally, didn't have any children and decided to serve roasted duck? Can you even imagine the horror and embarrassment my parents, or *any* parent, would suffer when a plate of food is set before their child at a friend's house and it is greeted with, "That looks disgusting. I'm not eating that." He also knew that one day we would grow up, leave home, and have homes of our own. The skills we picked up from him are invaluable.

Don't get me wrong, I make a mean chicken nugget, but my *boeuf bourguignon* is even better. I realize that not everyone has had the opportunity to learn from someone like my dad, but to borrow a phrase from *Ratatouille*, "Anyone can cook." If you can read, you can cook. I do believe Betty Crocker still has a cookbook out there. There's also a little thing called the Internet. There are several websites: Food.com, Kraftfoods. com, and Allrecipes.com are just a few that will take the ingredients that you have on hand, and help you plan a family-friendly meal in minutes.

Think about this: If the only thing our kids will eat are chicken nuggets, hotdogs, or mac and cheese with the occasional fruit cup thrown in, where's the balance of nutrition? We all learned about the food pyramid in health class in elementary school. There are four basic food groups, and although I just mentioned four different foods, I did not cover all four food groups. I have another friend whose son is seven years old, and he absolutely survives on chicken nuggets and tator tots. But, these have to be certain chicken nuggets—no off-brand—and the tator tots, Ore-Ida. She swears that if she even tries to put anything else on his plate, he gags; and the last well-balanced meal he had was when he was still in the highchair. So what does she do? She makes two dinners every night: one for him, and one for herself and her husband.

Okay, so maybe that's not such a big deal (I really do think it is a big deal, but for argument's sake, let's say for right now that it's not). If you have only one child, logistically you could easily microwave something relatively quickly. What if you have six children? No kidding, I have another friend (I am blessed to have a lot of friends who allowed me to survey them while writing this book) who, in fact, has six children. I asked her how she cooked dinner. She was a bit confused by my question. I rephrased my question a bit and asked, "Do you cook one thing for dinner, or do you let the children each decide what they would like to have?" It took her a full ten minutes to stop laughing! When she finally caught her breath, she said, "Are you crazy?! It would take ALL DAY just for one meal if I let each of them choose what they wanted for dinner! No. *I* decide. They can either eat it or not. That's their choice." Finally! Someone with some sense.

For the record, let me reiterate that although I do cook on average five nights a week, my children do not always greet my culinary experiments with an open mind and a willing stomach. At times, I am greeted with, "Uh, Mom? What exactly is it?" There have been nights when dinner didn't entirely turn out the way it was supposed to and the pizza delivery guy had to be called in to save the day...but the bottom line is that I tried, and they attempted to eat it. In all seriousness, what do you do when Junior refuses to eat? At our house, we kiss her (it's usually Emma) goodnight and put her to bed. She is not going to starve. Breakfast is served at six forty-five in the morning. If I'm going to go to the trouble to cook something, you better believe you are going to put out the effort to try and eat it. I'm not going to poison you. The food in front of you will not kill you. This is not a new perk that I discovered in the *1001 Ways to Slowly Torture Your Kids Handbook*. It's dinner. It covers the four basic food groups. It's good for you. Do us both a favor and eat it. If that's too much to ask, sweet dreams, I love you and will see you in the morning.

I know that may be a little bit more than some of you can handle. If you don't trust me, ask your pediatrician. She'll tell you. The kid won't starve. Eventually, your child will eat. Parenting is not for sissies. This is hard work. You must be consistent. I know I'm sounding like a broken record. If you waiver on this today and try to stand firm tomorrow, they will remember. And then they will push and push and push until they wear you down. Are you ready for that? Today the struggle is over green peas and roast beef, but later it's going to be over a ten-thirty curfew versus a midnight curfew or dating one-on-one versus groups of people. Stand your ground. Be the parent.

Finally, let me just ask you: Aren't you tired? I mean at the end of the day...if you work outside the home, once you've fought the traffic, picked up the kids, and made it home, do you really want to make more than one dinner? Do you want to even make *just one* dinner?! Hold everything if it happens to be baseball season, soccer season, or football season. Those weeknight practices will eat you alive. For those of us with girls—well, there's dance, gymnastics, and my personal favorite, art lessons twice a week. My head is beginning to throb just thinking of all of that. Realistically, if you are blessed enough to get off work by four o'clock, you could have your kids picked up by four thirty. Then you are walking through the door of your house by five o'clock, long enough to change clothes and hustle off to the ball field. Where is dinner? Drive-through? Homework is done in the vehicle.

Would you like to know a secret? Ten-pound packages of hamburger meat. That's my secret to hectic seasons of ball games and practices. I buy ten-pound packages of hamburger meat, brown it, bag it in one-and-a-half-pound bags, and freeze it. Voila! Dinner is half-way made. Hamburger helper is my BFF during game seasons! They can eat it in the truck from a plastic cup with a disposable spoon on the way to the ball field. It's cheaper than a drive-through. Throw some frozen peas into the pan while the noodles are cooking and you have a full meal in one pan! Frozen peas are my answer to a lot of things. Funny how I don't like to eat them, though!

On non-season nights, the schedule is basically the same. You still have to pick kids up. They will still have homework. At some point in time during the week, they will need to bathe. That's always a fun sport in my house—chasing the boys down. They don't seem to understand why they need to shower more than once every three days. It must be the Y-chromosome. The rest of the house still needs attention. Laundry will forever need to be done. I know for a fact in my house we have gremlins. It's utterly exhausting keeping up with the laundry. It never ends. Then, on top of all of these things...we still (many of us) have a spouse. It's during that special quiet time of the night—the kids are in bed, the dog is asleep by the couch, the TV volume has been reduced to a dull roar, and you are standing alone at the kitchen sink. You are finishing up the last of the dinner dishes, when who walks up behind you, and lays a gentle hand on your shoulder? Yep. Mr. Frisky. You know with one touch, one little touch, what that means. But you've just spent the last four hours in the kitchen making each one of your kids a different meal. You're bone-tired. In this corner of the Bark Park the kids reign supreme. They've won, and they don't even realize how great their victory is; however, I would wager you and your spouse are feeling how great your loss is becoming.

Power struggles come in all shapes and sizes: We have them over the food we serve our family. We have them over the in-bred need to defend ourselves and our property—whether that threat is real or perceived. Power struggles pop up between a husband and a wife when it comes to the way they will discipline and handle their children. All of these are elements in and of life. They are all just part of the Bark Park of life.

So, which pack will you run with?

Brotherly love is so sweet... What the picture doesn't reveal is Ethan swiping Elliott's pizza afterwards!

April, 2004,

I was forever putting the kids all together for pictures!

Who knows what, exactly, I was trying to accomplish!

The Shake Weight, Lipliner, & a Paint Can

. . . .

During the course of writing this book, I've undergone some extreme personal makeovers. I recently retired (although I am a bit young to use that word, it's truly the only word that fits) from full-time church work. I wanted to devote more time to the raising of my children and the writing of these books. I've mentioned before that I am a bit of a planner. I like to have things all laid out and know exactly what my next step will be. Well, choosing to stay home full-time was no exception. The only real trouble with that is the fact that life doesn't always turn out like we planned. I've worked outside the home on a full-time basis for the past four years, and on a part-time basis for the last seven, so I was really looking forward to some down time. I wanted to get back in the gym. Summer is always right around the corner when you live in Houston. It's never too early to start getting ready for the dreaded swimsuit season. Imagine my surprise, when here I sit, three weeks after my last day at "work," and I have not made it to the gym once. Not once. In twenty-one days, I've not had one spare hour to have to myself. *Why*? You may be wondering. I'm so glad you asked.

On April 21, 2011, I came home from work to find contractors in my house. I was surprised. Although, looking back on this, I really shouldn't have been. Jeff had mentioned, in passing, that he would like to make a few minor changes to the house. He listed several things that he would eventually like to upgrade: the floors in the upstairs bathrooms, for starters. At the time our discussion was taking place, both of the bathrooms upstairs were half carpet and half tile. I'm not quite sure whose brilliant idea that was. We bought this house already built, and when we moved in, I had a brand-new, two-week-old baby boy. That was not the ideal time for a remodel job! Well, I haven't been pregnant in a long, *long* time, so I guess he figured that it was safe to rip out the old flooring and lay down the new.

We also discussed replacing the carpet throughout the rest of the upstairs; after all, the carpet that was currently covering the floor was thirteen-year-old, builder-grade carpet that had survived three kids, numerous bottles and sippy cups, and countless contraband snacks, not to mention the hair dye stains contributed by my younger sister while she lived with us. It was time for new carpet. We also figured out that we were not using the house to its fullest potential. Let me explain: There are four bedrooms upstairs, two bathrooms, and one large playroom. As it stood, we were really only using two of the bedrooms, one bathroom and the playroom (obviously that is the only room big enough to house the Lego factory). We were dealing with a tremendous amount of wasted space. We needed to make some adjustments.

My "office" was upstairs and toward the back of the house. Jeff felt that it was safer to put me in the back of the house, as I am what some people call *creative* and others would call *a disaster*. The boys were, at one time, in separate bedrooms, but then my little sister moved in, thus putting the boys into one room. Emma has always had her own room. Can you say princess? All of this is important, I promise. So, basically Jeff and I discussed that we would like to further investigate our options for the house. I was in no way, shape, or form ready to move forward on a plan that was half-baked at best. I have to have a fully laid-out plan, an outline, and an end in sight. I was ill-prepared for the mayhem that I walked into that April day. Incidentally, the day was one week shy of my last day at work. Perfect timing...NOT!

As I walked in through my front door, I moved through a fine layer of dust that simply seemed to hang in the air. *Funny,* I thought to myself, *the house was clean when I left this morning.* This, however, was no ordinary dust. No, no. This was a supremely special kind of dust, a dust that not only hangs in the air, but gracefully settles itself in crevices and nooks and crannies that you didn't even know were there. This dust was the leftover remains of the pulverized tile from the upstairs bathrooms. The dawning of realization that my sweet husband had started the remodel project *without telling me* was flooding my senses. This also fell into the category of *101 Things Brainless Men Do to Aggravate Their Wives.*

I searched desperately for the filter that occupies the

space over my mouth and usually keeps me from blurting out the first thing that comes to my mind...but I couldn't find it. Instead I went straight for my husband, fire coming from eyes and smoke coming from my ears, "WHAT IN THE WORLD HAVE YOU DONE?!" I kid you not, when I tell you, *he did not know what the problem was.* "What? We talked about this, remember?" He could not understand, even as he led me upstairs to look at the new tile, why I would be upset.

Y'all, this dust was all over everything. Nothing had been spared. Nothing had been removed from the linen closets inside the very bathrooms where this destruction was taking place. I'll pause for a moment, for that to sink in. Clean sheets, clean towels, clean hand towels, clean washrags...were no longer clean, as the first person to attempt to use one of those towels to dry off with, would've only succeeded in creating a nice layer of mud on their bodies. Remember my office upstairs? Inside the closet of that room, which is inside the perimeter of the second bathroom, are the family scrapbooks. All of my children's baby books, family albums, countless pictures that have yet to be placed into albums...every last one of them covered in D-U-S-T...thick, nasty, dust. And still, Jeff was clueless. But that was okay. I took a deep breath, and focused on my last week of work. The house would have to wait.

Marriage is a constant learning process. Having a wedding ring placed on your finger is not the end of the game. We don't spike the ball and do our end-zone happy dance. Marriage is two different people figuring out how to live together in the same house without killing each other, or the kids. Medaling for gold in a knock-down, drag-out, scream-fest in front of the kids didn't seem to be the best option. I think back to when Jeff and I were dating. I never wanted to disagree with him because I was scared I was going to run him off. I always tried to look my best for him. I wanted him to be happy with the choice he seemed to be making. We eloped to Maui, and I have to admit that just before our sunset ceremony on the beach, I was a little worried that he would suddenly have a change of heart, change of mind, call it what you will—but the end result would be me, standing alone on a beach, far from home, with no husband.

March 14, 2000
Maui at sunset. Our wedding ceremony was something out of a dream.

Those fears were, of course, ridiculous. I've seen over and over again with people, who shall remain nameless, who have forgotten the thrill of dating their spouses. Their wedding ceremony was the end of everything instead of the beginning of something fabulous and exciting.

What does all of this have to do with remodeling? Or a Shake Weight? Or lipliner? I'm getting to that. Jeff and I have been married for eleven years, we have three great kids together, and we still have a wonderful time together. However, with that said, we still have trouble sometimes. There are days when I would just rather not get out of my jammies (can I get an AMEN on that one?), and days at a time go by when shaving *both* legs just isn't going to happen, but giving into those types of temptations too often, or for too long, will cause more problems than the pleasure a day of rest will provide. There's a popular myth floating around young marrieds today that once you get married, you can just let everything all hang out...and they do mean *everything*! Girls, I'm here to tell you there is nothing sexy or attractive about being so comfortable around your spouse that you forget to put your best foot forward. Boys, this goes for you, too. "Pull my finger" wasn't funny in fifth grade, and it's downright disrespectful as a married man.

One of the easiest "targets" for areas of improvement is the staying-in-shape area. I told you earlier, one of the things I was most looking forward to once I stopped working full-time was going to the gym. I probably should throw out a little disclaimer: I hate working out. I really do. I don't get any type of buzz or whatever the deranged folks who actually enjoy that type of torture get. I don't like it. I exercise because it's good for me, and working out allows me to keep up with my extremely active kiddos. I like being able to launch a football further than five feet for my boys. I like being able to pick my kids up and throw them across the pool. The benefits of working out outweigh the irritations. Now, having said that,

I'm also constantly on the lookout for the next best thing or way for me to work out with the least amount of effort.

Enter the Shake Weight.

What a letdown that was! So, I was watching TV one day, and this commercial came on introducing the latest and greatest in home fitness equipment (I use the term "equipment" loosely). This amazing little device is an arm weight. You shake it; hence the name—The Shake Weight. Anyway, by shaking this thing, a free-flowing weight inside the thing moves back and forth at a rapid rate of more than two hundred times per minute! In just six amazing minutes, you'll be on your way to supremely cut arms! No more fly-away, flappy wings that you try to shove into shirts or hide under sweaters! No Ma'am! With this miracle device for only $29.99, you'll be fit and trim for the summer!

Then, they showed all these women with beautiful arms and shoulders. Can you believe that? Well, I did...hook, line, and sinker. From the looks of the Shake Weight in the commercial, the free-floating weight somehow moved by itself. Um—WRONG! *You* have to shake it. You don't simply hold it while it shakes. You have to shake it. Brilliant. Don't worry, folks, my blonde hair is real. And for good measure, this thing is heavy; apparently that's where the *weight* part of the name comes into play. I bought it. I tried it. I discovered that six minutes is an eternity when holding an eight pound weight at chest level and trying to shake it with one hand. Forget that! I now use the Shake Weight as a New-Age and super-stylish door stop.

Besides, I've found a new and improved way of toning my arms: painting. The other part of my husband's exceptional idea (besides the bathroom demolition), was the redistribution of space throughout the upstairs. We both have a problem with waste. Our upstairs area qualified as wasted space. We sat the kids down and had a pseudo family meeting. We told them we were rearranging the upstairs and that meant they were all getting new rooms. Hooray! Yeah! Bonus! They were thrilled...until we told them they weren't getting new furniture. Bummer—came from Emma. A redistribution of space did not mean there had been a redistribution of wealth in this household. The layout of the second floor is absolutely perfect for our family. Do you remember the staircase (that Emma so lovingly STOMPS up and down)? Walk with me as we go on a little tour.

The stairs are not set in the middle of the house; they are off to one side of the living room, thus placing them on the outer edge of the second floor. As you reach the top of the stairs, there is a bedroom immediately to your right (this is the one the boys share) and another one directly in front of you (this one belongs to Emma). There is also a miniature landing, sort of like a computer nook at the top of the stairs. This small space doubles as a catch-everything-that-doesn't-have-a-real-home space. Oh, and somewhere beneath the Lego magazines, American Girl magazines, and Junie B. Jones books (that miraculously could not be placed on the bookshelf three feet away), there lies a computer desk.

To the left of the nook is a bathroom, and a bit further left is the step up into the playroom. Across the playroom (watch your step), you find yourself in a hallway. To your right is my office, and to the left is my sister's room, which has doubled as the makeshift guest room for the past year. (She'd left all of her bedroom furniture with us prior to her move to California, which worked out great for us! Apparently a complete bedroom suite wouldn't fit in the back seat of Honda compact!) Between these two rooms is a shared bathroom. It is this side of the house that has not been very well used. We were about to fix that.

Now, in order to move all of the children and the rooms around, the walls needed to be painted. Sounds easy, right? Not so much. All of the furniture in most of these rooms needed to move. Where to put it? Why, the playroom of course!

I have to pause right here for a minute.

Jeff and I really needed to talk more and more about this little project, and we decided that this would be fun (ha) to do together. The kids would still be in school through the month of May, so no chance of little "helping" hands. We could maneuver through the rooms quickly and swiftly and get this over and done in the short side of a week. Apparently, I had been inhaling too much paint. Naturally, when Jeff said *we*, I really thought that meant side-by-side, you help me and I'll help you, and, together-while-in-the-same-room, we'll get this done. Silly girl. The words "we" and "together" only meant in the same house.

Awesome.

So, this half of the "we" (which translated nicely to "me" or "I") moved furniture. This half of the "we" packed up books and moved them to the attic. This half of the "we" painted and primed...actually I primed and *then* I painted. Emma was moving out of her Care Bear laden walls and into her brothers' old room. She was unquestionably electrified at the mere thought. The hiccup? Her old room was the new guest room,

I painted Good Luck Bear on Emma's wall. He was supposed to be her companion, apparently until she married. I was wrong.

This is Bedtime Bear, who was on the wall above her bed.

This tree was painted by a talented artist named Janet when Ethan was an infant. For almost ten years, this tree has been upstairs. Cry.

This is what it looked like after two coats of primer! Sob!

and Care Bears—though cute and cuddly—didn't exactly scream elegant and adult.

They had to come down; actually they had to be painted *over*. I painted those Care Bears onto her wall six years ago. My sister and I mixed the paint and, painstakingly, with loving care, put those bears up. Now they were coming down. I could have cried. But what really made me cry was the fact that it took two coats of primer to cover the stinking things! Up and down, back and forth...who needs the Shake Weight? The Care Bears were effectively covered with primer, a stark contrast of white splotches up against the pale, creamy yellow of the walls. I would fix that later when I returned with the paint. Next, I moved into Emma's new room-to-be greeted by a ten-foot-tall, eight-foot-wide tree mural that had been painted on the boys' wall.

Again, two coats of primer, but as an added bonus with this room...I had to do the ceiling because naturally the tree's canopy stretched up and over half of the ceiling! I began formulating in my head the top ten ways to inflict bodily harm on a person (let's say a husband, just for giggles), using a paint can and a paint roller as your only tool. With every trip up and down the ladder, my mind circled around the fact that this was supposed to be *our* project. This was something *we* could do *together*. Being in the same house *did not* count as together! Inevitably, my mind would wander...

If I hit him with a full can of paint, would he know I wasn't liking my new role as Hired Help? Probably not. He'd probably think I'd slipped. Slipped...there's a thought...paint is slippery. If I poured it on the garage floor, and he happened to slip—nope, scratch that. If I poured paint in the garage...I'm the one who would have to clean it up.

Up the ladder, lugging the roller, losing my balance, trying with unsuccessful grace to stop myself from getting tangled in the rungs (I still have the bruises from that little mishap), I let some very colorful words go flying. You'd think that would've been my breaking point. It wasn't.

My breaking point came two days later, after I'd finished Emma's new room and was just about to begin painting her old room. As moms, we rarely get to finish anything in a day's time. Laundry, for instance, is never finished. Honestly, I don't know what the bottom of my laundry hamper looks like; I don't think I've ever seen it. The kitchen—is it ever *really* clean? I don't think so. As soon as you finish one meal, it's practically time to start the next one, or, at the very least, someone wants a snack. I was coming to terms with the "we" project turning into a "me" project with occasional supervision from him (he had been hearing the crashes and more colorful words that came from me as they filtered down the stairs and into his home office). I had been feeling guilty about abandoning my Shake Weight, and my gym had been sending little "We Miss You" cards, so this whole painting and moving furniture thing was working well for me.

I stood back, and looked at the room I'd just finished—floor to ceiling. It was done. I had finished something! I bent down, and found that I was a little slower to stand back up (going up and down a ladder twenty-two thousand times would've been easier when I was about ten years younger). I gathered my supplies and started to move back toward Emma's old room, which would eventually become the new guest room. I tipped my paint can into my paint tray and set my shoulders (and my back) for the task of painting another room. Enter husband, stage left.

I was finding my rhythm: dip, drip, roll; dip, drip, roll. Jeff walked into the room behind me, looked around at the progress I was making in this room, and said, "Wow. You're getting pretty good at this painting thing. Nice little workout, isn't it?" I agreed with him on the workout part, but I was leery about his motives. The grin he was displaying was a little too tell-tale. (Dip, drip, roll.)

"The upstairs will look nice when we get everything moved around, don't you think?" He asked me as he fiddled with the edge of my paint tray.

"Uh-huh." I said. (Dip, drip, roll.)

He cleared his throat. "Hey, I was thinking about having new windows installed upstairs...you know, since the upstairs is already torn apart. What do you think?"

I stopped in mid-roll. *What do I think?* My mind was having trouble processing the last thing he'd said. *New windows?*

Oh my stars!

Let me help you catch up to where I was in that moment: I was on the downhill slope of the upstairs switch-a-roo. Or so I thought. Having new windows installed just tacked on another two to three weeks of unrest in my house. I put my paint roller in its tray, sat down on the floor, leaned back against a freshly painted wall, and began to cry. I swear that tears to a man are like Kryptonite to Superman. He could not, for the life of him, figure out why I was so upset.

Pause.

. . . . . .

Do you remember what I said in the very beginning of this chapter? I said we needed to always put our best foot forward...

even after we get married. *Especially* after we get married. Well, this whole house remodel or switch-a-roo, call it whatever you will, was exactly that. The house was looking a little rundown. I love my house. It fits us. It suits our family. However, in the past nine years, as we've introduced new kids to the house, new dogs, and hosted too many pint-sized birthday parties to count, the house has achieved a tired look and a worn-out feel. Jeff was doing to the house (and for me, I might add) what I was trying to do with the Shake Weight.

Having babies and raising kids will wear you out. As moms, we, too, achieve that tired look and the worn-out feel. As parents (mothers), we have high-volume traffic areas, just like our carpets. For me, my high-volume traffic area is the pooch that I will most likely forever carry around my mid-section, unless I enlist the help of a talented and gifted surgeon. Y'all, having three babies in twenty-six months will stretch you out so that your skin has the exact same look and feel as the area of carpet that leads into your kitchen! There isn't really anything I can do about it. Sit-ups are from the devil. The Roman chair at the gym is Satan's favorite torture tool that women use to try to tighten skin that is happy to just hang. But, I still *try*. Why? Because I believe that not only am I charged with doing what I can to keep my body in good working order and condition so that I can literally keep going...BUT also for my husband. He deserves to still be able to see the woman he fell in love with twelve years ago. Even if seeing her means you catch only a glimpse through a veil of spit-up, diapers, and a blur of motion as she runs Child A and Child B to different practices.

I've worn my hair long for years. It's a style that I always seem to go back to. I didn't choose this particular hairstyle because it makes me look absolutely fabulous, but rather because it's easy. A quick twist and a clip or a rubber band works wonders when time to blow-dry has vanished. Recently, however, I cut my hair. My poor hairdresser hates it when I get into moods like that. She obediently cut off about seven inches of blonde hair, and turned what was left into a super-cute-and-spunky 'do. I will never be able to duplicate the style she has given me, but it looked great while I was in her chair! The first time Jeff saw me, he lost his mind...not because he was upset that'd I cut off all of my hair, but because he *loves* a short and sassy cut. Short hair is ten times more of a pain in the backside to fix everyday than long hair. Short hair requires a buffet of products to keep whichever style I managed to get it into that morning. But, do you know how much better I feel when my hair is fixed?

For starters, it means I've probably had a shower that day, and that's always a good place to start. When my kids were babies, it was very difficult to perform seemingly menial daily tasks. Tasks that I used to take for granted: brushing my teeth before noon, showering, getting dressed, etc. Once Jeff and I started having all of these kiddos, I had to become deliberate about those daily tasks. I want to encourage you to do something outrageous. I want to challenge you to let your baby cry while you hop in the shower and do a Ginsu shave on *both* legs today. Stick Junior in his crib or bring him in the bathroom with you, but the bottom line is: take a shower. Then, put on a little makeup, dry your hair, and get dressed. You don't have to dress to the nines, but just getting out of your jammies will do wonders for your mind. Your husband will think he's come home to the wrong house!

I know I've picked on us moms a little about our daily habits, but here's a tidbit for the dads. They make Shake Weights for men, too! Seriously, take a look at some recent TV sitcoms. There's a double-standard being portrayed on TV. I mean, we already discussed in chapter 1 that TV and movies have lied to us about the way a pregnancy should go...why should the parenting and the marriage be any different? I can think of a couple of different shows in which the wife/mother is svelte and smart and stunning. The husband/dad? He's a ginormous ignoramus. He's dumpy and overweight. He's not very intelligent. He's not the head of the family. The example he's setting is one of a slovenly lifestyle. Most men don't exactly struggle with the daily shower thing, most likely because they have to get up and go to work every day. Think about it for a minute, what would happen if a man stopped showering, stopped getting dressed, and *then* went into the office? He'd most likely be fired.

With that said, there are other areas of concern between a husband and wife that are simply not present between a boyfriend and a girlfriend. Take bathroom etiquette, for an example. I read an article in *Cosmo* many moons ago about things you should *never* let your man see you doing. Honestly, I don't remember most of the top ten, but the one thing that jumped out at me was: Never let your man see you brush your teeth. It isn't very graceful or elegant, but on the other hand it's a highly necessary part of a bathroom routine. Guys, take note. If witnessing us brushing our teeth is an off-limits area...what does that say about some of the bathroom stunts y'all pull? There needs to be respectful and healthy boundaries set around certain activities. For starters, close the bathroom door. Even though the husband is supposed to be the head of the house and the king of the castle—seeing him on his throne just doesn't scream, "I want you! Take me now!" Close the door. Be respectful of your wife's feelings and perhaps her sense of smell.

I realize not everyone has the ability to join a fitness facility, either because of financial obligations or proximity to your home, but the gym is not the only way to get some exercise. Remember those babies that probably wreaked a great deal of havoc on your body? They are more than just cute and cuddly. They are bona fide and certified *weights*. Notice I said *weights*... I did not put "shake" in front of it! Please do not attempt to use your baby as the new Shake Weight. This will not end well. Babies tend to spew like a can of Coke if you shake them around too much. You can, however, lie on your back and lift her over your head and then put her back on your tummy. She will think you are playing with her, and your arms get a terrific workout. Or you and your man can strap that baby in a stroller and strike out on foot *together* for a little evening walk around the 'hood. This is a double bonus...you both get some exercise and you get quality communication time because Peanut is occupied taking in all the sights around her.

Once we get married, the effort doesn't stop. It's a continual process. Being married with children really is about the same as living in a house that you are remodeling. It's loud. It's messy at times. And there is constantly something that needs your attention. Family life is the exact same thing. Now, back to my own little remodel job. I had to control my tears, and reassure my husband that I really was not crazy, but the chance of me arriving at that destination was fast approaching. I took a deep breath, and remembered that I wasn't talking to a first-rate imbecile, or a moron, or even someone who was deliberately trying to drive me out of mind. I was talking to my husband who loves me, and who genuinely wants to do nice things for me. It's just that at times like these we tend to speak different languages. I agreed to the new windows. And then I agreed to the new carpet. He promised to help me put the house back together, because at that moment in time, walking through our upstairs looked like we were auditioning for the series TV show, *Hoarders*. We literally had to climb over piles of stuff just to get from one side of the room to the other.

The children are now adjusting to their new rooms. The windows are halfway installed, and we both learned that a little communication goes a long, *long* way.

Jeff & I at a women's event in December, 2010

The Wrestling Match

L ast New Year's weekend, my family decided that we would
hitch up Nelson and venture out to one of the state parks
located close to our house for some rest and relaxation,
Texas-style. In short, we went camping for New Year's. This
sounded like such a great idea that another one of our close
friends wanted to go, so both families made the road-trip
up Interstate 45. The winters in southeast Texas make living here in the summer bearable. They are mild and, most
of the time, beautiful. In fact, we don't typically get hit with
the blistering cold that the rest of the country is hammered
with until February. The family we went with, the McCoys,
had two girls to match up with our two boys and one girl. We
both had campers, a bicycle for each family member, chairs
to sit in 'round the campfire, and a seemingly endless supply
of old-time country-n-western music coming from Mac's new
Christmas iPod. We were set up to have a great four days. The
Lake Livingston State Park is absolutely gorgeous. I believe that

no other place in the country grows pine trees quite like east Texas. They are tall and sturdy and mighty. Throughout the park, there are hiking trails and biking trails. It is simply beautiful.

I learned to ride a bike when I was very young. However, it has been too many years to count since I braved the two-wheeled mode of transportation, so as excited as my children were to scoot around pine trees and rocks and jump curbs like they were training to be the next extreme bicyclists, I was a bit more cautious. The McCoys were much better on their bikes than I was. So one afternoon, after we'd been there for a couple of days, and after all of the kids had gotten fairly comfortable with our surroundings, the kids wanted to go for a bike ride. I could see the mischievous look in Ethan's eyes; he was seriously thinking about some major daredevil stunts... Therefore, I was seriously thinking about letting the dads do this one alone. That was not going to be the case.

I had no idea what my sweet husband was up to, until he reached around behind me, and hollered to the McCoys, "Hey, y'all mind taking our kids for a bit?" He was grinning from ear to ear, like the Cheshire Cat from *Alice in Wonderland*. He gave Big Mac a guys-only wink-wink, just in time for our daughter Emma to see it. As if having a "locker room discussion" right in front of me wasn't bad enough...it gets better, or should I say, *worse*! Emma looked at her daddy and then at me, and then turned to the McCoys and said, "Oh, they're probably just gonna wrestle. They wrestle a lot." Mac and Lesli almost fell off their bikes. Honestly, if Jeff had not been holding me up, I probably would have slid to the ground. Mac was crying he was laughing so hard, and Lesli blushed slightly. Mac couldn't help himself. He had to ask, "So Emma, Mommy and Daddy wrestle, huh?"

"Yep," she said.

"Who wins?"

Emma smiled and rode her bike in a circle, not knowing the agony she was causing her mother or the satisfaction she was giving to her father... "Oh, Mommy wins. All the time."

Choke.

Okay, this brings us to a very interesting, intricate, and vital part of life for a married couple with kids. Let's talk about sex. We can't really survive this parenting thing without a little hand-to-hand communication with our spouses. I know you know how to do this... I mean, you had kids; even if you adopted your precious little ones, the act of *trying* was still involved. Life with kids is hard. Let's face it, when you've been spit-up on, thrown-up on (yes, there is a difference), done twenty-seven loads of laundry and you still cannot see the bottom of the hamper, made three complete meals and numerous snacks...having some quality couch time with your honey probably isn't ranking very high. There are a couple of factors that play into that decision. For one, you're flat out exhausted, and having sex takes some energy. And two, Baby Vomit #5 isn't the most appealing perfume on the market, so you may not be feeling particularly sexy. I received an email in my inbox several months ago that speaks to this very predicament. Allow me to paraphrase (this is not word-for-word):

Housework is typically seen as a "woman's job," but one evening Fran arrived home from work to find that the kids had been bathed, one load of laundry was in the washer and another one was in the dryer. Dinner was on the stove and smelled delicious, and the table had been set. Fran was amazed!

It turns out that Fran's husband, Fred, had read an article that said wives who work full-time and had to do their housework were too tired to have sex.

The night went great, and the next day, she told her office friends about all that had taken place at home:

"We had a wonderful dinner. Fred even cleaned the kitchen. He helped the kids with their homework, folded all of the laundry and put it away. I really enjoyed my evening."

"But what happened afterward?" her friends wanted to know. Fran giggled, "Oh that... Fred was too tired."

Go ahead and laugh, but this is all true. In the last chapter, I talked about the necessity of maintaining your physical health. Now I want to talk about the incontrovertible truth of the importance of maintaining a healthy sex drive after the kids make their appearance. In the beginning of most relationships, we don't sit down and make a list of the jobs or roles we will each play. For instance, after Jeff and I got married, we didn't take a pad and a pencil and make our list of who does what—with "always initiating sex" falling into his column. Nowhere does it say that the initiator must always be your husband. In fact, to keep things lively, you would go to him before he has a chance to come to you. Folks, sex is a gift, and it is to be shared and enjoyed, but only within the boundaries and confines of the marital bed.

There are so many stumbling blocks in this area of marriage and parenting that will trip up couples. The most obvious obstacle is the children themselves. The sheer time that they require of their parents makes it almost impossible to conform to the traditional timetables and locations. Now, don't worry, I'm not about to get X-rated on you, but we are going to talk about some things that will be uncomfortable for many people. It still amazes me that Jeff and I were able to have as many kids as we did in the short amount of time that it took to have them. New parents—check that—new *mothers* don't ever sleep. We can't sleep, because in the beginning the baby doesn't sleep...well they don't sleep at *night*...the days are a completely different story!

Now, I nursed my children. I realize that isn't for everyone, but for mothers who make that choice, nursing tends to complicate sex. I nursed my babies on demand. When they cried or acted like they were hungry, I fed them. Nursing is quite a bit different than a bottle. With the bottle, you pretty much always know how much Junior is taking in, but with the breast—no dice. Just about the time I would get one kid to sleep through the night, I would deliver a new one. In short, I had someone touching me all day long. I was either holding one who just wanted "up," or I was nursing one because it was time, or I was pregnant with one, so touching any part of me could, at any time, result in projectile vomiting.

So when Jeff would come home and try to be frisky or loving or just want a little attention for himself, often times *I* was the problem. I just didn't want another person touching me. My body was not my own. I was an incubator or a cow—a.k.a., automatic milk dispenser. On the occasion that I was in the mood when he was in the mood, my body would present a different set of issues. (Disclaimer: If you're a man reading this book, I apologize for the detail you are about to get about a woman's body.) Did you know that the same hormone that releases a mother's milk is the same hormone she produces during sex? Kind of weird, but true. Many nursing mothers have the ability to feed half the neighborhood until her milk is fully regulated, and that can take a long, *long* time, so whenever Jeff wanted to "wrestle," often times he got more than he bargained for. For the longest time, all I could picture was the milk ads from magazines, "Got Milk?" Why, yes, yes I do! The automatic response of my body to let down the milk had sort of a drowning effect on the mood...literally. We had to learn to work around it.

Sex is very different for a man and woman. We view it differently. I once heard women compared to Crock-Pots and men compared to microwaves[2] when it came to their readiness in the bedroom. Truer words have never been spoken. Girls, can I tell you I don't have a magic "on" switch. A Crock-Pot takes time to warm up, whereas a microwave heats up instantly. Most men at the mere mention of sex are raring and ready to go. With women, that's not always the case. I cannot "rev up" at the drop of a hat, especially after holding babies all day, feeding babies, and changing diapers. I need time to warm up to the idea. However, when you are dealing with little bitty ones, time is a commodity you don't often have access to. I've said over and over again that we have to be intentional and deliberate in our parenting. We do. There is no way around that. But we also have to be exceptionally deliberate and intentional when it comes to relations with our spouse. It is very easy to get so caught up and so derailed in the details of daily life that we forget about each other. Please do not let this happen to your marriage.

I have particularly fond memories of my grandparents. Both are gone now, but as a kid, I spent a great deal of time with them: Mimi and Papa. There wasn't any other place I would rather be. Mimi and Papa were married for over fifty years before they were called home. One of the earliest memories that I have of the two of them happens to be from a Memorial Day trip to the lake. My entire family (and I do mean entire—Mimi and Papa, aunts, uncles, cousins, parents, then of course my sisters and I) would travel about an hour and half north of Austin to Lake Buchanan, and spend the four-day weekend in these little old cabins right on the water. We would rent two cabins (think of a duplex); each cabin was one room and two double beds, one bathroom and a little kitchenette. All eight of us grandkids, plus the really cool aunt and uncle, would hunker down in one cabin while the rest of the grown-ups stayed in the other.

I remember walking into the grown-up cabin one morning and seeing my grandparents still sleeping on their air mattress. They were snuggled so close together, at first glance you would've thought it was only one person laying there. That's how they did things. They did it together or not at all. Well into their sixties, they still chased each other with the fervor and vigor of a newlywed couple.

I knew from the moment I saw them sleeping on that air mattress, I wanted *that*. I wasn't going to settle for anything less. They were married in the 1940s. They saw war. They had poverty. They had too many mouths to feed and not enough money to go around. Yet still, their love, their *hunger* for each other survived. They were deliberate. It probably didn't hurt that they were both fairly stubborn and strong-willed Germans!

Mimi & Papa were married over fifty years.
They were always this close, always together,
and always in love!

I took that one memory of them, plus all the others I collected through my years with them, and carried it into my marriage with Jeff. I knew what we could be, if only we went after it and fought hard to keep it. Marriage is hard. Marriage with kids is almost impossible—if you are not willing to stand your ground and fight for what you have. How do we do that?

Believe it or not, your family life does not revolve around your children. Now, how many folks did I just upset by that statement? Honestly and truly, your family life should not revolve solely around your kids. You and your husband should be the center of each other's eyes. I'm not in any way, shape, or form telling you to ignore your children, but I am telling you to be careful about how much emphasis you place on them.

There have been many times when I looked at Jeff, as sweet and wonderful as he is, and wanted to throw something hard and heavy at him (a paint can for instance). I'm sure he would tell you the same thing about me. However, it is precisely that passion, that spunk, and that sheer grit and determination that makes us ache for each other when we are apart.

Eventually our kids (your kids) will grow up and leave home. That's the goal of proper parenting. You take these babies, you love them, you teach them, but in the end—they move out. (We have ten years, two weeks and three days until our last one is out...in case anyone was wondering.) What will be left is an empty house, and a husband and a wife. The burning question is: Will that husband and wife have any idea who the other one is? The answer, if you've spent the last twenty years putting your kids first in everything and placing them above your spouse is: No, you won't. We cannot let that happen.

I know that in today's day and time, there is a great deal of emphasis on the family bed. This is a crock! The family bed will quickly move from "family" to "Junior and Mom" while Dad retreats to Junior's abandoned bedroom. As I've said, in our house, we have two stories, and the children's bedrooms are all upstairs while the master bedroom is located downstairs and through the living room. In short, we are far from our kids. Now that they are older, this is not such a big deal, but when they were newborns and infants, this was a *huge* deal. We had a cradle in our room, so that the new baby could be close to me for the first weeks of their life. This was practical, as they were up every couple of hours, and it was best for the rest of the house. Let's face it, getting up with a crying baby is hard enough; having that one baby wake up another child would have been more than I could handle!

Once our babies started rolling around, it was time for the cradle to go in the attic, and the baby to be introduced to his or her new room. This was about the time I started writing names on all the baby monitors I had beside my bed. Jeff and I were on the same page from the get-go. Life was hard enough without purposefully adding obstacles to separate us. The time it takes to care for these kids and the time it takes for him to work was stress enough, so we didn't need, nor did we *want*, a child lying *in between* us at night. It made no difference as to whether sex was involved or not, we wanted—no, check that—we *needed* to be able to reach over in the night and simply touch each other.

We learn by what we see. Sure, we can tell our children all day long until we are blue in the face what they need to do, or how they should act, but the fact of the matter is that they learn best by what they see. Case in point: me and my grandparents. I don't remember them ever sitting me down and telling me the secret weapon to having a long, successful, and happy marriage. I picked that up from *watching* them. What kind of an example are you setting for your kids by letting them get in between you and your husband every single night?

There are exceptions to every rule. I'm not stupid. And I'm not a monster. Kids get sick, and they need to be beside you. They have bad dreams that won't go away by turning on a light; they need to be comforted by the touch that only comes from Mom or Dad. I get that. Kids also need boundaries, and they need to be taught and shown to respect your boundaries as parents. There are very specific boundaries that have been set around the marital bed. Your children are not invited to cross those lines. They are, however, encouraged to witness the protection offered by those boundaries via the lock on the bedroom door.

Allow me to explain. I have some friends; they have been married for fifteen or so years. They have two children: a boy who is thirteen and a girl who is almost ten. To this very day, neither one of those children sleep in their own beds. Their daughter sacks out in her parents' bed, right between Mom and Dad, and their son? Well, he's around the corner on the couch in the living room. Their lives revolve around their kids. Granted, they are some of the most involved parents I've ever seen. She volunteers for everything under the sun at both of her children's schools. He coaches everything from baseball to soccer to gymnastics. But what about them as a couple? That's a completely different story. Now, let's look at the opposite side of that spectrum.

I'm going to get letters because of this chapter, I can feel it.

Ethan was introduced to his first babysitter when he was six weeks old. I "borrowed" her from the nursery at church. I knew her and I knew her family. She had helped me over that summer as I taught (in a very pregnant state) vacation Bible school. I felt comfortable leaving our son with her. It was the first time Jeff and I went out to eat since he was born. I worried about him through the entire meal. I called four times in a time span of an hour and a half. When we arrived back home, and found him asleep in her arms, the house still standing and no visible signs of fire damage, we hired her again two weeks later.

The next time she came over, we ate dinner and saw a movie. I called once. Jeff and I began to enjoy each other as a couple. Obviously, we were enjoying ourselves because a couple of months later, I got pregnant with Emma! It is imperative that you maintain your identity as husband and wife as well as playing the role of Mommy and Daddy. Your family will suffer into the next generation if you fail in this area. But, no pressure.

Something else Jeff and I have done is take mini-vacations without the kids. I know that statement right there is cause for some of you reading this book to hunt me down, but hear me out. Can I ask you a question? I want you to think about this before you answer. Do you like your spouse? I'm almost certain you love your spouse, but do you *like* your spouse? Can you imagine yourself going away for a weekend with just him? No kids, no friends, just the two of you. Would you have anything to talk about, other than the kids? What would you do? Where would you go?

Often times when Jeff has to go somewhere for a couple of days on business, I will go with him. We will get his mother to come over and watch the kids, or call one of our sitters to come in and help out just so the two of us can have some alone time together. It is wonderful, marvelous...I don't have all the adjectives to describe it. We are able to reconnect on levels that are amazingly refreshing for our bodies and our spirits. We live just outside of Houston, and a couple years ago, we had the opportunity to spend one night in one of the super-fancy downtown hotels. Y'all, we totally jumped on that! It was just for one night, and it was really just down the road from home, but for the fun we had together...we may have just gone to the other side of the world! *But what about the kids?* you may be wondering... *What will they feel like when Mom and Dad leave? Will they feel abandoned? Rejected?*

No, no, and no.

The kids will be fine. Most kids love hanging with new people: especially if they've been exposed to them from early on. These date nights, dinners, and little overnight getaways are warm-up exercises for the marathon of an actual, out-of-town, long haul, Mom-and-Dad-only vacation. Through the years, Jeff and I have been blessed with the resources to go away for some nice vacations *alone*.

The time we spent together has been priceless.

Five years ago, we went to Italy for two and a half weeks. My heart longs to go back there. We left the kids with three different rotations of grandparents while we were gone! I'm not sure who had more fun between us, the kids, or the grandparents! I realize that Italy is one of those once-in-a-lifetime dream destinations...I get that. Aside from the sights that we saw and the places that we visited, Jeff and I were in a foreign country where we had

Jeff & I at the Leaning Tower of Pisa in Italy, 2007

just the two of us to rely on. Neither one of us speak Italian. Although, we figured out *vino* (wine) fairly quickly! The memories we made together, and the wrestling matches we scored! Wow! Those were just a taste of what's to come after the kids leave home, but none of that will be possible if we don't keep in touch with each other in the interim.

I have the privilege of speaking to a lot of moms' groups, and one of the most heart-wrenching things I hear from women is a lack of respect both *for* their husbands and *from* their husbands. Intimacy is not merely a physical act. In fact, according to the Merriam-Webster dictionary, the word "intimacy" means *innermost* or "something of a personal or private nature."[3]

How difficult will it be to touch your spouse's body if you've wounded their heart? So many couples today are dealing with respect issues that it just breaks my heart. Respect is a two-way street. Being from the south and the west puts me into a very unique category as far as respect goes. Jeff and I are trying (some days are better than others) to teach our boys that girls go first. Is it always fair? No, it isn't. But sometimes life isn't fair, and girls should go first. Girls are special above all else in creation, and they need to be treated accordingly...even sisters. Respect, or rather *disrespect,* between a husband a wife takes on a myriad of different faces.

Many of the groups I speak to are MOPS groups (Mothers of Pre-Schoolers, see www.mops.org for more information). This is a fabulous organization that affirms and builds up the mothers of children ages kindergarten and younger. And in these groups, the women are divided into small groups or tables. The discussion inevitably turns to husbands. The banter that goes back and forth between these women makes me wonder why they got married in the first place!

Listening in: "My husband never gets up with the baby... never helps with the kids...never picks up his clothes...always

plays golf on the weekends…never defends me to his mother…
always makes fun of my cooking…"

Then there's my personal favorite, when the conversation
turns to sex: "I'm not giving him any until he learns to help
me with the kids!" Ouch. Y'all, our men are not five-year-olds
who need to be given a time-out. Sex is not a tool, or worse,
a *weapon*. Sex is a gift. The only way we will even begin to see
that is when we begin to see each other the way we used to,
and that may mean looking at each other through the pre-baby
goggles. Ladies, our husbands are not big, stupid lumps. They
have a purpose and a plan. They have feelings. It's just that the
two of us really do speak in different languages. We were each
designed and created to complement each other; we are like
puzzle pieces. Sometimes we will be like polar opposites, but
in the end, we should always come back together.

Can I challenge you to take some action? When you find
yourself in the middle of a husband-bashing session, will you
stop, take a breath, and try to say something edifying about
your spouse? One kind word has the power to redirect an
entire conversation gone amuck. Sounds easy, right? What if
you happen to be really miffed at your man? I just happen to
have a story:

A while back, Jeff had to go out of town for business to
San Antonio. Now, San Antonio is about a four-hour drive
from Houston. This trip was a last-minute type of thing that
I thought, if he really wanted to, he could've gotten out of.
He went ahead and made his plans to go, leaving behind one
supremely put-out wife. One day into his trip, he called and
asked me to drive out and join him. We could walk on the River
Walk, tour the Alamo, and do all the goofy things that tourists

do... Oh, and we could celebrate my *birthday*. I proceeded to tell him exactly where he could put the Alamo, as I'd already seen it, and if he was so keen on seeing the River Walk then maybe he could just jump in and go for a little swim. I wasn't having it. I hung up. I was fairly pleased with myself that, just like riding a bicycle, the ability to spit fire is something that also returns to you in the blink of an eye. My stunned husband did not try and call me back. I, however, picked up the phone and called a friend for a congratulatory conversation about what a bonehead my man was.

Now, the girlfriend I called has been my friend since we were eighteen years old. She knows me better than I know myself. She has seen me at my best and seen me at my absolute worst. Somehow, through all of that, she still loves me. Naturally, she's the one I called. I relayed the conversation to her, feeling quite proud of the way I handled the situation. I was totally unprepared for her response.

"Are you out of your mind?" she asked me, once I stopped long enough to take a breath.

"Excuse me?" I asked, somewhat taken aback.

"Are you out of your mind? Why would you say those things to him? D—he loves you. He provides for you—"

"Yeah, but, he went out of town for my birthday, like I wasn't important."

"And that gives you the right to 100 percent disrespect him to *him*, and then to *me*? You need to be on your knees thanking God He gave you this man. You could be without a husband."

And with that last statement, I was sorry. The friend I was talking to is unmarried. She doesn't have a husband. She doesn't have the gift that I have. She saw something so clearly, so unmistakably plainly, that when she pointed it out to me, her voice quivered with anger. I expected the anger, though not directed at me. I immediately called my husband back and told him I would be in San Antonio the next morning. I apologized to him for the things I'd said to him and for the things I'd said *about* him. Y'all, it is crucial that we build up our spouses. The world and just about every other aspect of society will do their level best to tear them down. It will be up to us to protect them.

The Wrestling Match.

As our kids have gotten older, we have had to come up with more evasive terminology for what is actually going on behind the closed and locked door of our bedroom. Most recently we tell them we are "talking." But the more I think about this, the more I like "wrestling." Do you know what wrestling actually is? I'm really pretty much nothing more than a word-worm. I'm a big nerd who likes to know what words mean and find out where they came from. Ever since our "wrestling" story broke this past New Year's, the word "wrestling" has been on my mind. As I've walked through some of my last points with y'all, I think it's time I share some of the things that I've learned throughout the course of this last year. You can determine for yourself if "wrestling" is the right word for the horizontal dance between husband and wife. I think you'll be surprised. The Merriam-Webster online dictionary defines "wrestling" as "a sport or contest in which two unarmed individuals struggle hand to hand with each attempting to subdue or unbalance the other."[4] How's that for accurate?

Have you ever been knocked off-balance by your man? I have. It's awesome. During this whole, let's-flip-the-house-on-its-side-and-turn-it-inside-out thing, I had the opportunity to watch Jeff take some things apart, and then subsequently have to put them back together. He focuses so intently on whatever task he's working on that it truly takes my breath away, and makes my knees go weak. In short, I'm completely knocked off-balance.

I watched him take down a ceiling fan in one room and switch it with another one in a different room. I was mesmerized just watching him, and now even thinking about it, it makes me smile. Do you have a moment like that that you can draw from? Somewhere between the diapers, the dinners, and the ball games...do you have a spare moment that you can pull a memory of your man and travel back in time and let that memory push your button?

If you don't, put the kids to bed early tonight, call your mother-in-law to watch them or put in a movie for them upstairs, and get busy making that memory today! Be intentional about your spouse. In this world of technology in a millisecond, let him know you are thinking about him. Shoot him a spicy text message at three o'clock in the afternoon. Chances are, he will not dawdle on the way home from work. Do you remember those long kisses goodnight that you used to share before you got married? Try dusting one of those off, and send him off to work with that to think about. Rev his engine first thing in the day. Then keep it on a slow hum all day long.

We don't have to spend three weeks in Italy drinking red wine, eating cheese, and making love in foreign hotel rooms to recreate the lost romance in our child-ridden marriages. We have all the tools we need right here at home. All you need is your imagination, some pre-planning, and an open and willing heart. Try looking at each other as Man and Woman, instead of just Mom and Dad. If you take the bull by the horns every once in a while, the rewards will be awesome.

Girls, think about all the energy and attention we put into our babies. If we spent a third of that energy on our men, I guarantee you the divorce rate in this country would go down. It's time we take our families back! That starts with our marriages. If you were to ask any one of my children if they felt like they are loved, adored, and treasured by their parents, they would look at you like you were nuts, and then answer: "Of course." But if you ask them, when it comes to Daddy, who comes first, you or Mommy? Hands down, their answer would be: "Mommy!"

Our children know they are loved. We tell them. We hug on them. We kiss them. We take care of them. But the number one way they know they are loved is by the way Mommy and Daddy love each other. Jeff and I have provided—are providing—them with the foundation of trust and solidarity to last them a lifetime. This is how life is supposed to work. This is how husbands are to treat their wives. This is how wives are supposed to treat their husbands. We are a team. And we are just getting started.

Ethan, Emma, & Elliott,
Summer 2006

Squirrel!

I have three kids. I know you know that; I'm almost certain I've mentioned that before. My kids are young and they are close together age-wise. To make things easier on myself and my husband, we decided early-on to have the same set of "house rules" for everyone. That seemed to be the logical way to do this rather than having different rules for each kid.

As I was walking through the upstairs the other day to return a Nintendo DS to its proper resting place, I came across a root beer can. An *empty* root beer can. This can was in an odd place; it was upstairs. Soft drinks do not live upstairs, nor do they get to visit the upstairs, and once the new carpet arrives next week, an accomplice to these visiting soft drinks will have some medieval type punishments brought down upon them. As it was, I picked up the lone root beer can and continued my journey to return the stranded DS. I had only made it a couple of feet when I noticed a pile of clothes sticking out from under the couch in the playroom. *Odd*, I thought quietly to myself. Clothes don't typically live under the couch.

I set down the root beer can and the DS on the side table, and bent down to collect the lost clothes. I found socks, undies of varying owners, a bathing suit, and a pair of pajama bottoms. While on my hands and knees I also came across a pair of scissors that really and truly is supposed to reside in the kitchen. I stood up, put the scissors in my back pocket, scooped up the clothes, nabbed the root beer can and the DS, and headed to the bathroom where the laundry chute is located. In order to open the linen closet door, I had to set the root beer can down on the counter where it instantly stuck like glue due to the overwhelming presence of Colgate Plus toothpaste for kids. I rolled my eyes, switched the DS to the other hand, opened the door, and attempted to drop the clothes down the laundry chute. No dice. The laundry chute was blocked.

Now, I'm no expert at laundry, and it is true that I typically wait to do laundry until Emma is forced into Spider-Man underwear before I will do a load of clothes, but I was standing in a bathroom located on the second floor of my house. There was NO WAY the chute was that full. I began to pull items out one at a time. Towel after towel, after sheet after sheet, jeans, then a board game (not sure what they were trying to prove with the game), another towel, the spare comforter from the guest room (come to find out, that's where the majority of the root beer went—I made a mental note to check the bed for remnants of more root beer)... Eventually clothes started tumbling down the chute and I could hear the happy sounds of them hitting the hamper below. I also heard the conspicuous sounds of Legos plinking against the sides as clothing and towels made their way down. I returned my attention to the lost pile of clothes that had started this scavenger hunt of sorts, and the now-thoroughly abandoned DS some thirty minutes earlier. Into the chute went the clothes, down the ramp (now unobstructed), and into the hamper. I turned to pick up my companion, a.k.a., the DS, and I reached for the root beer can and promptly found it cemented to the counter. I needed supplies to unstick it.

Still holding the DS in my hand, I walked down the stairs to the kitchen, set the DS on the counter, opened the cabinet under the sink and retrieved the necessary supplies for unsticking the root beer can from upstairs. Back upstairs I headed. After another thirty minutes in Emma's bathroom, I decided that since I was already up there, and I had all of my supplies, it made good sense to try and attack the boys' bathroom as well. Forty-five minutes later, the job was completed. However, on my way through Ethan's room, my nose detected the unmistakable aroma of corn nuts. I felt like a bloodhound as I sniffed in and around the nooks and crannies of his room trying to locate the source of the smell.

Bingo! Jackpot! Call it what you will, I hit pay dirt. Evidently, Ethan had gotten hungry in the night, and had gone downstairs to snag a bag of corn nuts, taken them upstairs, and proceeded to eat them *in his bed*.

Gross...was the first thing that came to my mind. Ethan sleeps on the top bunk of a set of bunk beds. Terrific.

Naturally, I had to change the sheets. When I pulled the fitted sheet from the mattress, corn nuts flew through the air. Happy thoughts of what I was going to do to my firstborn after school filled my mind. I put clean sheets on his bed, picked up all of the corn nuts from the floor, gathered my cleaning supplies, and began making my way to the stairs. I was halfway across the playroom when...OUCH!

Legos are the bane of my existence. I never step on them when I have on shoes. I find every single spare part when I'm barefooted. It's amazing.

I dropped the sheets, put down the cleaning supplies, and began picking up Legos and depositing them into their home-base tub. Then, I bent down to gather sheets and supplies, got all the way down the stairs and into the laundry room, started the sheets in the washer, and began making the return trip through the living room to the kitchen... Pause... I saw the Sunday paper. There are coupons in the Sunday paper. I did need to make a run to the grocery store.

Plopping down on the floor and thumbing through the ad section, I found that I was in need of some scissors. I remembered seeing some upstairs, so I got up, returned to the upstairs, and began searching for the lost scissors. They weren't in the playroom, but I did find a lovely collection of naked Barbie dolls that belonged in Emma's room. I gathered those and headed toward my daughter's room. I was thinking maybe she had scissors. She always has stuff like that.

So, I put away the Barbies, and looked for the scissors; I couldn't find scissors, but I did find a glue bottle that had been knocked over. I began to visualize what I would do to *her* once she came home from school.

I went back downstairs to get the necessary equipment to remove glue from the inside of a drawer. I realized that the instruments that I needed for that job should be in my bathroom. On my way through my bedroom, I saw that I forgot to make my bed. I stopped to make the bed and pick up the spare socks that Jeff had left on the floor on his side of the bed, so, I carried those to the laundry basket in our closet. Perfect! The basket was full.

I sat down and began to sort clothes. I heard the bell on the washer, indicating that Ethan's sheets were ready for the dryer. So, I grabbed a load of whites and headed to the laundry room. Transferring one load from the washer to the dryer, I started another load in the washer. Then, I headed back to the kitchen area for a time check. It was almost time to grab the kids from school; I saw the dogs' food bowl was empty, so I went to the garage to fill the bowl and take it back to the kitchen, where I saw the DS from that morning that never got put away in the first place!

I grabbed a hold of it, determined this time to put it where it belonged, and headed back upstairs. As I rounded the corner at the top of the stairs, from the corner of my eye, I saw the contraband root beer can still sitting on my now-clean bathroom counter.

I honestly think I'm losing my mind.

I reached for the can, half expecting it would move away from me, thankful that it did not, and I continued my journey to put away the DS.

Mission accomplished. With the DS securely placed in Elliott's room, the root beer can in-hand, down the stairs I went, until I saw the newspaper sitting on the living room floor... I walked over to the paper, set down the root beer can, glanced up at the clock, and ran out the door to grab the kids from school.

Upon returning home with all of them and walking into the door of the house, Ethan reached into my back pocket, pulled out the scissors that I had put in my pocket for safekeeping six hours earlier, and handed them to me.

Emma picked up the root beer can and threw it away.

And Elliott folded up the paper and carried it to Jeff's office.

Have you ever had one of those days?

With kids, we have those days a lot. I feel as though I don't ever really get anything done, but I have a lot of practice walking in circles. Now, I told you that story to tell you this one:

We are moderately well-acquainted with kid-friendly movies in our house. Go figure. I am particularly fond of kid movies that offer adult humor for Mom and Dad; little added bonuses like that make the whole let's-watch-this-movie-again-and-again-and-again-and-again thing, well, tolerable. One of the best movies to provide this dual role in recent history was *Up*. If you'll permit me to take us to the end of the movie with the talking dogs, I'd be grateful. The talking dogs are chasing Doug (the other talking dog, apparently in movies things like this can happen, and no one blinks an eye) via airplanes. The dogs are flying around and around and they are closing in on our heroes.

All of a sudden, Russell (the kid in the movie) yells out "Squirrel!" The dogs crash into each other due to the mass chaos caused by each one of them looking for the prized squirrel. They took their eyes off the prize of our heroes for an instant, and in that second, all was lost. Squirrels in a dog's world represent the end-all, be-all of walking, talking, squeaky toys. They love them. They cannot get enough of them. They can almost never catch them, but that doesn't stop them from trying. Even the most trained and obedient dog can be derailed by a squirrel.

Over the past eight chapters, I've shared with you my goal for raising happy, healthy kids that will one day grow into balanced and productive members of society. My way of doing things is not the only way, but it is what seems to be working for Jeff and I. Before I leave you, I cannot let you walk away thinking that I don't chase my own "squirrels." Remember the root beer can and the DS? It seriously took me all day to get those two objects in their rightful places—and even then, my kids had to help out! That was a definite "Squirrel!"

I've been looking back over these memories of mine, and I must admit that writing them down like this is the closest thing to a diary that I have. People used to see me out with all of the kids; after the initial shock wore off and the immediate fear that I was not deranged for taking all of these babies out in public, they would ask me, "How do you do it?" Plain and simple, I draw my strength from Someone else.

Jeff and I were both raised in Christian homes. That is a belief and a faith that we both carried into our marriage, and are now carrying into our parenting. It's totally true that Jeff and I eloped. We chose to do that for a couple of different reasons, the first being that my parents were not fired up about shelling out a small fortune for the type of wedding I wanted, thus setting the precedence for my three younger sisters. The second reason is simple: Our wedding was between God, Jeff, and me. Having people around would've been nice, but the fact of the matter is that the promise we made to each other and the promise we made to God is the one that counts. It did not matter if his family was all the way on board with me yet... It did not matter what my mother said about weddings in general.

The only thing that mattered is the fact that Jeff and I stood before God and promised on His Word to love, honor, and cherish each other 'til death do us part. We meant it.

Do you think having three babies in twenty-six months was easy? Let me answer that for you: It so totally was NOT! But you don't get to jump ship midway through just because this may not be exactly what you signed up for. We knew from the beginning that we would never have to fight this alone, "A cord of three strands is not quickly broken," (Ecclesiastes 4:12, NIV). It was—check that—it IS God plus the two of us. We will withstand the fight.

From the meager beginnings, I moved us through the roller coaster rides and the ups and downs of parenting. My mind keeps circling back to our time at Disney World...the *first* time. We waited for an eternity to see those princesses. In reality, we are waiting right now. Even when we are going through the extreme busyness of our days, we are *waiting*. Let me explain.

There was a time in our history, man's history, when we were waiting. Everything was in a holding pattern. All of creation seemed to be holding her breath. God set the stars in the heavens and called them each by name. He set the motion to the ocean, and placed each creature in a habitat especially designed for each species. Then He created man. Out of the dust of the earth, God Himself formed man. He blessed the man and gave him a helpmate: God gave man...*woman*. Naturally, through the course of time, we mucked and muddied all of that into a great, big, unholy mess. (So much for God's perfect creation.)

But, God had a plan. Here's where the waiting comes in. We had to wait for it. We had to wait for *Him*. In God's own time, when He knew that the time was right, He would send His own Son to us. He, Jesus, would live down here, in the mess we've made; He would wait with us. He would teach us;

He would remind us of the way that God would have us live. I thought about this *after* I got back from Disney World... Honestly, while I was waiting in line, all I could focus on was singing the next song and wondering how high my kids could count! Hear me out on this. Psalm 27:14 (NIV) says, "Wait for the LORD; be strong and take heart and wait for the LORD."

Do you remember what Elliott did when he saw Cinderella? Oh my stars! He ran to her. He couldn't wait any longer. He bolted from me and ran to her! She received him, even if she was slightly surprised by the amount of force in that little body! There will come a day when our wait here will be over. It's true.

You see, Jesus *did* live down here with us. He *did* teach us. He also *died* for us. He died in our place, took the punishment that would be ours for the mess we'd made, so that ultimately, we would not have to. That's not the end of the story. No! He died on a cross, but as He is God, the grave could not hold Him. He rose and ascended back into heaven to be with God our Father. Now, y'all, I've told you all of that to tell you this: Those Disney princesses were held in a throne room of sorts. It was a big deal to get to go and see them. We waited for what seemed like an eternity, and then the kids' joy overflowed and they were rewarded with hugs all around from the princesses.

Well, we are still waiting right now. We are waiting while we carpool. We wait while we grocery shop, and while we run to the bank. We wait while we help with homework, bake cookies, make costumes, and watch ball games. Make no mistake, there will come a day when your wait, and my wait, will be over. *This* is not our home. "But our citizenship is in heaven" (Philippians 3:20, NIV). We will be greeted in heaven by our heavenly Father, and His arms will be wide open. Run to Him, be ready to embrace Him, and don't be shy… I promise you one thing: God is *way* more sturdy than Cinderella!

You may be wondering why I'm dropping all of this on you now. Why didn't I pepper the rest of the book with the reasons why and all of my hows? As you may have guessed, there actually IS a method to my madness. I *so* wanted you to enjoy the book in its entirety, and please don't misunderstand me, I'm not insinuating that this chapter is not worth the read! I simply wanted to give you a condensed place to look for all of my structure, without the need for an index. This chapter will be your overview and quick reference guide…sort of like a Cliff's Notes of *The Mommy Diaries*.

As you can imagine, raising three itty-bitties at the same time wasn't always fun and games. There were days when all I could think about was getting to their morning naps. I remember thinking, *Why is this so hard? Am I making it more difficult than it has to be?* Well, the answer, simply put, is: No, I wasn't making it harder than it had to be. We live in a fallen world. We are going to have trouble. In fact, Jesus, Himself, tells us in the New Testament from John 16:33 (NIV), "I have told you these things, so that in me you may have peace. In this world you will have trouble. But take heart! I have overcome the world."

Honestly speaking, how many times have you felt like you were the guest of honor at the Mad Hatter's tea party? Perhaps you were seated in one of those brightly colored spinning teacups? Now, not every day is going to be an uphill climb to the summit of Mount Everest. At least, I pray that it is not. The Mad Hatter had an uncommonly unique gift in the way he viewed his world. Sure, things were often upside down and inside out, but he saw those things as *blessings*. Have you ever thought about that? He was delighted to live in a world that was a little "off" from the way others saw things. He had a great deal of fun that way. Parenting can be, and should be, the exact same way! I've looked back on all of the situations, issues, and events that my family has (miraculously) lived through over the last ten or so years, and I've found, through the simple process of writing them down, that Jeff and I have done things a bit differently than a lot of other people would. That's okay. *You* will raise your kids differently than we have, and that's okay, too. The one area that will be consistent across the board is *trouble*. We will all have trouble. Our kids will step one toe over the line, no matter how far out we stretch that line. Boundary after boundary will be exceeded. We cannot hope to raise well-balanced and productive adults unless we enlist the help of Someone who has been there first.

Look at it this way: God the Father was the first Parent ever. He created Adam and Eve in the Garden of Eden. He gave them everything they could ever have hoped for and dreamed of. He set boundaries around them. He set boundaries around them to protect them and to keep them safe. He was their Parent; they were His children. The first thing He told them was "don't." "And the LORD God commanded the man, 'You are free to eat from any tree in the garden; but you *must not* eat from the tree of the knowledge of good and evil, for when you eat of it you will surely die,'" (emphasis added, Genesis 2:16–17, NIV). And what did Adam and Eve do? They ate from the very tree they weren't supposed to! So, if God had trouble with His children, doesn't it stand to reason that we would have trouble with ours?!

I promise this picture was NOT staged! Emma
really did feed her little brother an apple. The
only thing that would've made this any better
would have been for Elliott to have been
shirtless, too!

I realize that thought right there is enough to make us all
throw our hands up in the air, and scream "I QUIT!" I mean, if
God could not control His kids, how in the world will I be able
to handle mine?!

Hold on. I think it may be time for a time out.

"Squirrel!"

I want to reiterate that the little stunt that Adam and Eve
pulled in the Garden with the apple or the orange or whatever
fruit they just couldn't live without, did not catch God off-
guard. I want to say that again: The Fall *did not* take God by
surprise. He wasn't sitting up in heaven, when all of a sudden
He felt a mighty rumble beneath Him. He didn't need to send
a messenger down to Earth to find out what was going on. *He
already knew* what the outcome was going to be. Before the

foundation of the world was laid down, God knew Adam and Eve would slip up, and the plan to send Jesus was already in motion.

Picture this: You make for your children a nice, hot, steaming, nutritious bowl of yummy spinach (ick—I don't really care for cooked spinach). Now, you have also gone to the trouble to make an ooey-gooey, fudge-laden, whipped-cream-topped-with-sprinkles ice cream sundae. You offer both to your children at the same time. Which dish will they choose? Duh. The sundae, hands down. Now, you knew that before you handed both dishes to your kids. It's virtually the same thing with God. He knows which path we will walk before the path is ever laid out in front of us. With us, His children, He's done something amazing and unexpected: He's installed in us a free-will chip. We get to *choose*. We have the choice to choose good or choose evil.

Comforting, isn't? There will be days when trouble comes barreling at us from all sides and all directions, so much so that we will not even be able to defend ourselves. We will feel like we are stuck in a bumper car that has run out of juice. When that happens, think about the fact that Jesus offers His peace: "Peace I leave with you; my peace I give you. I do not give to you as the world gives. Do not let your hearts be troubled and do not be afraid" (John 14:27, NIV).

Did you know that the Bible tells us more than three hundred times not to fear? God knew we would be weighed down by fear. Therefore, over and over again, He tells us throughout the pages of Scripture *not to fear*, or *fear not*, or *do not be afraid*. There is one "fear not" (or some derivative of that) reference for every day of the year. How's that for planning ahead?

I'm always simply blown away by the relevance of the

words of Scripture, too. Nine times out of ten, the passage I'm reading is exactly what I needed to hear at that exact moment in my life. How does He do that? I have a theory. I had an original plan for this book. I did. I thought it would only take me about six or eight weeks to write this thing. I'm pretty sure there's a joke in there somewhere: If you want to make God laugh, tell Him your plans! But, my plan for this book was to just hammer it out; I mean how hard could it be? I've got three kids, they are constantly getting into trouble and/or situations, so I would just take all of things that they were doing, and jot them down. I figured that moms everywhere would be able to relate. That was my plan. That was also in January.

We are now knocking on June's door: I've made several trips to the doctor for sick visits with all three kids—ranging from bronchitis to a weird, exotic kids' skin rash that required African beetle juice to get rid of (seriously—I'm not making this up); executed a women's conference; planned a summer retreat; spoke to numerous women's groups; lived through a fairly massive home renovation project; oh, and had the awesome privilege of visiting two of Texas' finest hospitals for two different kids. Life doesn't often allow you the time to accomplish all that you'd hoped. However, the goal for this book has not changed. I'm still praying that the people who read my rantings and, at times, ramblings, will find some humor, comfort, and solace nestled within the confines of its pages. As much effort and energy as I'm putting into this project of mine, eventually it will be dated material.

The one thing that I've included in this book that will outlast any bit of advice or any tidbit of information are the verses plucked right out of the pages of God's Word. How can

I be so sure? Those sacred words have stood the test of time thus far...oh, and God, Himself, says so. "For the word of God is living and active. Sharper than any double-edged sword," (Hebrews 4:12, NIV). The Word of God is alive; it has the breath of God in it, therefore, we can use it with a confidence and with a power unlike anything else we've ever experienced. And believe me, when it comes to raising kids, we are going to need all the help we can get!

. . . . . .

The other day I watched a documentary on the National Geographic Channel about life inside the womb. I thought it was going to be very interesting. It really only succeeded in thoroughly freaking me out. The program I was watching was following the pregnancy of an elephant. That's right, I said *elephant*.

Elephants are pregnant for about two years. Looking at the spectrum of the animal kingdom, that's a really LONG time to invest in one single pregnancy. I mean, there are no guarantees that *one* baby will survive. Granted, the elephant is bigger than most any other animals in the desert or the jungle, but still...two years? Eyow! As if being pregnant for two years wasn't bad enough...oh wait, *I* was pregnant for two years! Anyway, back to elephants... As if being pregnant for two years wasn't bad enough, they deliver a two-hundred-and-fifty-pound newborn! Ouch! Here's the really mind-blowing thing: Those babies stay with their mothers for about five years! The mother selects "babysitters" to help her watch her new baby. Female elephants typically run the herd. Why am I telling you all of this? I worry that sometimes today's modern woman (for lack of a better term) feels that she must operate on her own.

We have been sold a bill of goods, and girls, we've bought it hook, line, and sinker. If we cannot do this parenting thing all by ourselves, and work outside the home and keep our houses in pristine condition and have the energy and sex-drive of our twenty-one-year-old counterparts...well then, we just aren't up to snuff. All of that is a lie...one...giant...big...FAT LIE.

In fact, here's a new (actually it's an old) little nugget for you: It takes a village to raise a child. We cannot do this thing alone. It is imperative that we enlist some help. I mentioned several chapters ago a little something about the MOPS International organization. I encourage you to go online and find a group that is close to you. Finding a group of women who are walking down the same diaper-strewn path that you are on will help you get out of bed each and every day. The women that are in these groups understand what it's like to get out of your house in the morning with an oatmeal hand-print on your bottom. They know that this season's newest fragrance really is Baby Vomit #5. They understand what the Big Spring Shave is because during the winter months they simply do not have the energy, strength, or inclination to attempt shaving their legs.

There are three undeniable blessings that come from join-ing a MOPS group. The first: they have childcare. You can put your precious bundles of joy in the care of qualified profes-sionals who will love on them and rock them for two hours while you go and enjoy some grown-up, mom time. The sec-ond: they have food. Your group will feed you. Something hot and delicious. In short, twice a month, you will eat a breakfast that does not consist of cold rice cereal and strained pears or mushy Cheerios. And finally, MOPS International is built on the solid foundation that Jesus Christ is God's own Son, and that He died on the cross, was buried, and rose again...all to save us from our sins. I have to admit that I found my calling into the leadership of women through MOPS. I cannot raise these kids alone. I never could. I couldn't do it when they were babies; I certainly cannot do it now that they are growing older. I met my very best friends through MOPS. It was all in God's plan to have me there. And He has a plan for you, too.

He will help you with your sanity; He will help you with your discipline. Did you think that while I was writing the chapter about feeding a fish, that I did that for my own giggles? No, no, no. It is for their own good. I must do everything that I can to raise these children up to be productive members of society. How can I expect them to be good members of society if they have no understanding—no comprehension of right and of wrong—of consequences? Our children must be taught obedience. I'll admit this is something I struggle with a bit. I want them to obey—there's no struggle with that aspect. In order to achieve obedience, we must be consistent. Rules must be put in place and they must be followed. When they are not followed, consequences must be followed through with. Not merely empty threats. We cannot sit back and continually say: "If you do that one more time..." "If you do that one more time..."

Our children are incredibly smart. They will know in an instant whether or not we are bluffing. I remember one night we were sitting at the dinner table, and one of the boys asked me why I always told them that they had to obey me. Why did I use the word *obey*? Y'all, if you get nothing else out of this book, I want you to hear this: I told them it is essential for them to obey me because I have to obey God. You could have heard a pin drop at our dinner table. I went on to tell them this: "Believe it or not, you three do not belong to me, nor do you belong to your daddy. Y'all are on loan to us from God. God is letting Mommy and Daddy borrow you. While we have you, we promised that we would teach His Word and His ways. We would teach you to obey Him and teach you to obey us... Just as we have to obey God, so, too, do you."

Their eyes were so wide, they looked like saucers. Emma asked, "Momma, *you* have to obey?" I affirmed that yes, I do. I asked them why they thought I made them hold my hand in a parking lot. The answers were pretty straightforward: "To keep us safe, so we don't get run over." I assured them that those were all true answers. To this day, Elliott (big surprise) still fights me on holding my hand while walking through parking lots. I have to repeatedly remind him, and his brother and sister, that my vantage point is higher than theirs—meaning I can see things that they cannot see. Point blank: I'm taller. I can see cars coming, and the cars can see me. They understood that. I can see dangers coming because my eyes look out from a higher place. They were all following me up to this juncture. Then Ethan asked, "So why do you still have to obey God? Aren't you a grown-up?" Yes. I am a grown up, but I'm still God's child, and I still need direction from Him. Just as my eyes see things that are higher than my children's, so God's eyes are higher than mine. He can see hidden dangers that I cannot. Therefore, when we pray and we ask Him for something, and the answer is "no," remember there is always a reason. There may very well be a danger coming around a corner that you cannot see. But the eyes of God see everything. No one likes to be disciplined, but it is necessary, so that we all grow up to be good, productive members of society.

So, when your children ask you why they have to be disciplined or corrected, offer them this: "As you endure this divine discipline, remember that God is treating you as his own children. Who ever heard of a child who is never disciplined by its father? If God doesn't discipline you as he does all of his children, it means that you are illegitimate and are not really his children at all. Since we respected our earthly fathers who disciplined us, shouldn't we submit even more to the discipline of the Father of our spirits, and live forever? For our earthly fathers disciplined us for a few years, doing the best they knew how. But God's discipline is always good for us, so that we might share in his holiness. No discipline is enjoyable while it is happening—it's painful! But afterward there will be a peaceful harvest of right living for those who are trained in this way" (Hebrews 12:7–11, NLT). It won't make the punishment, the discipline, the correction, or whatever you choose to call it, any more pleasant or bearable, but perhaps it will help you both to see the prize at the end of the race.

· · · · · ·

While I have your attention on a touchy and difficult subject already, I may as well push the envelope a bit further and skip ahead to the relationship between husband and wife. We all live in a day and time when the divorce rate is higher than the marriage rate...or so it seems. Every time I turn around, someone else is getting a divorce. My heart is breaking for those couples who just can't make it work. Divorce is an epidemic. However, it is not a new epidemic. The CDC (Center for

Disease Control) will most likely not be issuing any updates or warnings as to how to protect you and your family from the devastating and far-reaching effects of this disease. There is no vaccination for this. No one is immune. The only protection we have is our grit, determination, oh, and a little help from the Almighty.

I was looking forward to writing the chapter about the wrestling match. I hope that translated well for y'all. I don't want there to be any misconceptions about the relationship that Jeff and I have. Don't panic, we really and truly do have a great marriage. But, I don't want you to read this and think that everything in our house is always full of hearts and flowers and little love notes. It isn't. That's not realistic for anyone. We have issues just like anyone else. What makes us different is how we deal with those issues.

Did you know that there is a power-struggle going on between husbands and wives? I'm sure you knew that. I'm sure you can feel that from time to time within the walls of your own homes. Have you ever wondered why? Why would God design a union to be everlasting, yet so difficult to peacefully coexist? The answer goes back, *way* back...all the way back to Genesis and starts with something like, "In the beginning..."

When God got busy forming the universe, He merely spoke everything into existence. He spoke and the sun began to shine. He spoke and the waters parted. He spoke and creatures filled the sea, the air, and the land. However, the pattern of creating broke when He made man. When God made man, He *sculpted*. He placed the man, called Adam, over everything that the LORD God had made. "God saw all that he had made, and it was very good" (Genesis 1:31, NIV). Now, all the creatures of the world: air, land, and sea—they all had mates, but the man did not. So God did something else utterly amazing. He put the man to sleep, removed a rib from his side, and formed *woman*. Well, we've discussed the Fall; they ate the fruit that they were not supposed to eat from, and here comes the consequence. If you've ever wanted to know why you and your man lock horns, look no further than Genesis 3:16 (NIV), "To the woman he [God] said, 'I will greatly increase your pains in childbearing; with pain you will give birth to children. Your desire will be for your husband, and he will rule over you.'"

Now, I've read that passage for years and years, and I never really thought the second part was all so bad. Quite honestly, I was more concerned with the whole pain-in-childbirth thing. I thought that having desire for my husband would be a good thing, and I really couldn't figure out why that would be part of the curse associated with the Fall. Here's where having a strong affinity for words comes in handy. The desire mentioned here is not desire as in sexual desire, meaning eyes only for your man. No girls. This desire is something much darker, much more sinister. The desire we are talking about here is one to usurp your husband's authority. The reason we sometimes go toe-to-toe with our husbands is a direct result of the Fall. This is all part and parcel of the curse. God designed us to be a helper to each other, to complement each other, but then sin entered the world and shot that all to pieces.

We must resist the urge to always have our own way. I know that sounds like the hardest thing in the world. Who doesn't want things to roll their way? I know that I personally like it when the sun is shining on me and everything is coming up roses, but do you want to know a secret? My husband is the exact same way. Someone, somewhere, has to give. We are to give in to each other, putting their needs above our own.

At times, this will be exceedingly difficult. But the benefits far outweigh the negatives. How do we do this? I mean most of the time husbands and wives speak different languages.

Brace yourself, here comes an electrically charged word: We have to *submit* to our husbands. I know that makes a whole bunch of people cringe. This word, *submit*, has been misunderstood for years and years. Let me assure you that to submit to your man does not mean to roll over, play dead, and be a doormat to him. The word *submit* means to defer to another's judgment or opinion. We submit to each other in all relationships in one way or another. For instance, When you call your girlfriend and you are discussing plans for lunch and a movie, and you want to eat at an Italian restaurant and she wants Mexican food, you defer to her opinion and go eat Mexican food. You've just submitted your will to hers. That doesn't make you a doormat. It simply makes you aware of her feelings, opinions, and needs. It's the same with our husbands, in a slightly different way. God placed our husbands in the position of protector over us. Our man is supposed to be the head of the house. He is supposed to lead us, guide us, and make the majority of the decisions for us and our family. That was the original plan.

However, way back in the Garden, that's not how this went down. The serpent got to Eve. He coaxed her and convinced her to eat from the forbidden tree. Eve stepped outside of her safe boundaries set in place by God, and Adam failed to do his job...which was to protect her. Because of his mistake, and because Eve made such a monumental and devastating decision on her own without the aid or consent of her husband, married life would forever be shaken. We, as wives, will always try to seek the dominating role over our husbands and usurp his God-given authority. Ladies, we must resist that urge! We must try and remember Ephesians 5:22–23 (NIV): "Wives, submit to your husbands as to the Lord. For the husband is the head of the wife as Christ is the head of the church..." I know that sounds really hard to do. Don't think for a moment that our men get off scot-free.

They don't. God lowered the boom on them pretty hard, too. Adam failed miserably in his role as guardian over Eve in Garden of Eden. His charge was to look over and care for everything in the Garden...including, and *especially*, his bride. He did not do that. While the crafty serpent was working his magic on Eve, where was Adam? Was he off somewhere else? No. He was standing right *beside* her. He just stood there. He did nothing. He was, in short, a coward. His job was to stand between her and the enemy. His job was to protect her from evil forces, even if that meant protecting her from *herself*. Genesis 3:6 (Contemporary English Version) tells us, "The woman stared at the fruit. It looked beautiful and tasty. She wanted the wisdom that it would give her, and she ate some of the fruit. Her husband was there with her, so she gave some to him, and he ate it too."

He was right there! Because of his cowardice and his inability to defend, his punishment in the curse would be the constant power-struggle between husbands and wives throughout the ages. Good news, right? Well, just as wives are charged with submitting to our husbands, our husbands have a fairly hefty load to carry, too. I'll admit, I get bogged down in the whole submission thing. I like things the way I like them. I don't always want to bend my will to Jeff's. Sometimes I don't think it's fair.

Take a look at our husbands' job description. You see,

Scripture is meant to be read together. It is meant to flow. A lot of folks really like to pick it apart and make it say whatever they want. However, this is dangerous ground. Power-hungry men can very easily throw out the "wives submit to your husbands" and leave it at that, but for the rest of the story, you must keep reading. Yes, it's true, we are to submit or bend our will to theirs, but reading further in Ephesians we see what they are to do. Ephesians 5:25–26 (NIV) says, "Husbands, love your wives, just as Christ loved the church and gave himself up for her to make her holy, cleansing her by the washing with water through the word." Wow. Our husbands are to love us in the same manner as Christ loved His church. Christ *died* for His church. That's how far our men are supposed to go for us.

So, what does all of this really have to do with parenting our kids?

Raising happy kids starts with *connected* parents.

When parents are thoroughly connected to each other spiritually and physically, the family, as a whole, will reflect that. There will always be trouble. There will always be rainy days. But the sun will always come back out. Sure, I walk in circles, I chase squirrels, I don't remember what the bottom of the laundry hamper looks like...but does that really matter? No, it doesn't. My kids are happy. My kids are safe. They have boundaries (that they try to cross every day). My husband comes home to me every night. We laugh over our mistakes, and try to learn from the goof-ups. And because life is not like it is in the movies or on TV, we both carry a notebook...

Surviving parenting is not for sissies; nor is it for the weak or faint-hearted. But along the way, we will have some great laughs!

Right after the Texas Longhorns won the 2005 National BCS Championship, Elliott slept with the DVD of the game! He watched it non-stop for weeks!

Ethan & Emma completely tuckered out from camp play all day!

Daddy & Ethan catching some zzz's on the couch.

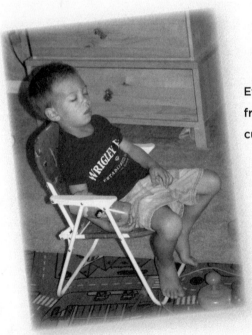

Ethan wiped out in front of the TV, sippy cup in-hand, snoozing!

Notes

1. Associated Press, "California Woman Held for Duct-Taping Toddler," Fox News, February 18, 2011, http://www.foxnews.com/us/2011/02/18/california-woman-held-duct-taping-toddler/.
2. Author and Speaker, Gary Smalley.
3. "intimacy," Merriam-Webster.com, last accessed October 21, 2011, http://www.merriam-webster.com/dictionary/intimacy.
4. "wrestling," Merriam-Webster.com, last accessed October 21, 2011, http://www.merriam-webster.com/dictionary/wrestling.